Becoming a
Teacher Leader

Becoming a Teacher Leader

From Isolation to Collaboration

Lee G. Bolman
Terrence E. Deal

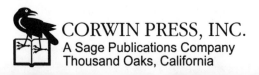

CORWIN PRESS, INC.
A Sage Publications Company
Thousand Oaks, California

For information address:

Corwin Press, Inc.
A Sage Publications Company
2455 Teller Road
Thousand Oaks, California 91320

SAGE Publications Ltd.
6 Bonhill Street
London EC2A 4PU
United Kingdom

SAGE Publications India Pvt. Ltd.
M-32 Market
Greater Kailash I
New Delhi 110 048 India

Printed in the United States of America

Library of Congress Cataloging-in-Publication Data

Bolman, Lee G.
    Becoming a teacher leader : from isolation to collaboration / Lee
G. Bolman, Terrence E. Deal.
        p.   cm.
    Includes bibliographical references (pp. 83-85).
    ISBN 0–8039–6087–5
    1. Teaching. 2. Educational leadership—United States.
3. Teachers-student relationships—United States. 4. Classroom
management—United States.   I. Deal, Terrence E.   II. Title.
LB1025.3.B65   1994
371.2—dc20   93–36370
                                                                            CIP

94 95 96 97 98   10 9 8 7 6 5 4 3 2 1

Corwin Press Production Editor: Marie Louise Penchoen

Contents

Acknowledgments

Many of the ideas in this book were stimulated by our research on school leadership under the auspices of the National Center for Educational Leadership (NCEL) and by the work of the Harvard School Leadership Academy (HSLA), both funded under grants from the U.S. Department of Education. Our friends in Washington, David Stevenson and Ron Anson, have been steady sources of both support and constructive criticism, and we are very grateful to both of them. We also owe much to our colleagues in NCEL and HSLA for their ideas and encouragement. Ideas from Susan Johnson's work on the school as a workplace and from Carol Weiss's work on decision making are echoed in this book. Reva Chatman's doctoral thesis, "Fresh Roses," a novel about beginning teachers, and Tracy Kidder's wonderful chronicle of teacher Chris Zajac in *Among Schoolchildren**, gave us both inspiration and a deeper understanding of classroom life. Pam Burish, Donna Culver, William D. Greenfield, Jr., Thomas P. Johnson, Ann Lieberman, Gayle Moller, Emmanuel L. Paparella, and Carrie Sedinger provided very helpful comments and suggestions on an earlier version of the manuscript.

* Excerpts from *Among Schoolchildren* by Tracy Kidder. Copyright © 1989 by John Tracy Kidder. Reprinted by permission of Houghton Mifflin Company. All rights reserved.

Our spouses, Sandy Deal and Joan Gallos, provided more than the usual support and love—without which writing would be dreary if not impossible. Each also brought her own special expertise. Sandy Deal's extensive experience as a clinical psychologist greatly strengthened the teacher-student interactions in the book. Joan Gallos used her work on gender issues in the classroom and in adult life to provide us with many helpful insights; Joan's feel for good storytelling also strengthened this work in many ways. Many educators in the United States and abroad have been *our* mentors and guides, and we have learned more from them than we can ever say.

LEE G. BOLMAN
TERRENCE E. DEAL

About the Authors

Lee G. Bolman specializes in leadership and organizational change. He is the author of three books and numerous articles on leadership, organizational change, and management development, including *Reframing Organizations: Artistry, Choice, and Leadership* (written with Terrence E. Deal). Bolman has been a consultant to corporations, public agencies, universities, and public schools in the United States, Asia, Europe, and Latin America. He has taught for more than twenty years at the Harvard Graduate School of Education, where he has served as Lecturer on Education and Director of the National Center for Educational Leadership. Beginning in Fall 1993, he will be Marion Bloch Professor of Leadership at the University of Missouri, Kansas City. At Harvard he also served as educational chairperson of two executive development programs, the Institute for Educational Management and the Management Development Program. He has been director and board chair of the Organizational Behavior Teaching Society, and a director of the NTL Institute for Applied Behavioral Science. Bolman holds a B.A. in History and a Ph.D. in Organizational Behavior, both from Yale University.

Terrence E. Deal specializes in the study of organizations. He has written several books and numerous articles on organizational issues. His most recent book, co-authored with Lee G. Bolman, is *Reframing Organizations: Artistry, Choice, and Leadership* (1991). *Corporate Cultures* (1982), co-authored with Allen Kennedy and translated into ten languages, was an American bestseller and won international acclaim. Deal is a consultant to businesses, hospitals, banks, schools, colleges, religious orders, and military organizations in the United States and abroad. As Professor of Education and Human Development at Peabody College of Vanderbilt University, he teaches courses in Organizational Theory and Behavior, Symbolism, and Leadership. He serves as Co-Director of the National Center for Educational Leadership (NCEL), and Senior Research Associate at the Center for the Advanced Study of Educational Leadership (CASEL). Deal previously taught at the Harvard Graduate School of Education and the Stanford School of Education. He holds a Ph.D. in Educational Administration and Sociology from Stanford University.

Introduction

What does leadership have to do with teaching? Isn't leadership what principals and superintendents are hired to do (regardless of whether they do it very well)? Some teachers don't see the connection between teaching and leading, and some scholars agree with them. One day while writing this book, we encountered a paper outlining the duties of teachers. It stated flatly that leadership skills "are entirely unnecessary for good teaching" (Scriven, 1991). If true, that would be discouraging news about the prospects for a book on becoming a teacher leader.

As luck would have it, on the very same day we also came upon a lovely list of the "shared characteristics of excellent teachers," and the first item on the list was "a vision for children." Because vision is currently the first item on almost everyone's list of the characteristics of effective leaders, there is definitely a connection there. But leadership is more than having a vision; it is having a vision that can be shared with others. Note the following dialogue from Tracy Kidder's *Among Schoolchildren*. It's a conversation between a teacher, Chris Zajac, and Clarence, one of her students. Zajac is a confident, committed, and experienced teacher. Clarence arrived in her classroom with a mountainous "cume" (cumulative record) and a reputation for driving teachers crazy. He immediately

1

showed signs of living up to his reputation in Zajac's class. Only a few days into the fall term, Clarence was doing almost none of his assignments. Zajac kept him after school to talk:

Chris sighed, got up, and walked over to Clarence.

He turned his face away as she approached.

Chris sat in a child's chair and, resting her chin on her hand, leaned her face close to Clarence's.

He turned his farther away.

"What's the problem?"

He didn't answer. His eyelashes began to flutter.

"Do you understand the work in the fifth grade?"

He didn't answer.

"I hear you're a very smart boy. Don't you want to have a good year? Don't you want to take your work home and tell your mom, 'Look what I did'?"

The fluorescent lights in the ceiling were pale and bright. One was flickering. Tears came rolling out of Clarence's eyes. They streaked his brown cheeks.

Chris gazed at him, and in a while said, "Okay, I'll make a deal with you. You go home and do your work, and come tomorrow with all your work done, and I'll pretend these two days never happened. We'll have a new Clarence tomorrow. Okay?"

Clarence still had not looked at her or answered.

"A new Clarence," Chris said. "Promise?"

Clarence made the suggestion of a nod, a slight concession to her, she figured, now that it was clear she would let him leave.

Her face was very close to his. Her eyes almost touched his tear-stained cheeks. She gazed. She knew she wasn't going to see a new Clarence tomorrow. It would be naive to think a boy with a cume that thick was going to change overnight. But she'd heard the words in her mind anyway. She had to keep alive the little voice that says, Well, you never know. What was the alternative? To decide an eleven-year-old was going to go on failing, and there was nothing anyone could do about it, so why try? Besides, this was just the start of a campaign. She was trying to tell him, "You don't have to have another bad year. Your life in school can begin to change. If she could talk him into believing that, maybe by June there *would* be a new Clarence. (Kidder, 1989, pp. 10-11)

Chris Zajac faced a classic *leadership* challenge, as she struggled to find and express a vision to sustain hope and possibility for her as well as Clarence. If she could do that, she would pull off something very special. Teaching and leadership are both about infusing life and work with passion, meaning, and purpose. In his classic book on leadership, John Gardner summarized our view succinctly: "Leaders teach. Lincoln, in his second inaugural address, provided an extraordinary example of the leader as teacher. Teaching and leading are distinguishable occupations, but every great leader is clearly teaching—and every great teacher is leading" (Gardner, 1989, p. 18).

Leadership, like teaching, is essentially a relationship and a process of mutual influence between leaders and those they hope to lead. Every move that Zajac made was influenced by the responses that she got from Clarence. Good leaders, like good teachers, are as good at listening and sensing as they are at persuading and teaching. What distinguishes leadership from other kinds of relationships is that, when it works well, it enables people to collaborate in the service of shared visions, values, and missions. At their best, teachers, like other leaders, shape relationships that make a measurable difference in others' lives, even though those differences may be hard to assess and may not come to fruition for years after the fact. Kidder puts it well:

Teachers usually have no way of knowing they have made a difference in a child's life, even when they have made a dramatic one. But for children who are used to thinking of themselves as stupid or not worth talking to or deserving rapes and beatings, a good teacher can provide an astonishing revelation. A good teacher can give a child at least a chance to feel, "She thinks I'm worth something. Maybe I am." (Kidder, 1989, p. 513).

It is not easy. As a teacher, you continually face the challenge of figuring out what is going on—in your classroom, in your school, and in your community—as well as getting a handle on what you can do about it. You know from experience how hard that can be. The everyday world of the classroom presents a complex series of challenges, puzzles, interruptions, and assorted frustrations. Sometimes they are punctuated equally by moments of joy, laughter, energy, and exhilaration. The dynamics inside your classroom are tough enough. What makes it even harder are all the problems and pressures that originate outside its walls—directives from the principal, complaints from parents, district policies, state regulations, and breakdowns in families and communities. More and more, teachers are asking or being asked to assume leadership roles in these wider circles.

To make sense of all this, you need to organize vague, confusing, and messy symptoms of life in schools into a meaningful pattern so that you can choose the right thing to do. In diagnosing the situations that you encounter every day, you draw on the experience that you've acquired over a lifetime. It's given you a set of lenses that you use to define and frame reality for yourself inside and outside your classroom. Even if your lenses or frames are sometimes off target, you still have to use them, because they give order to confusion and let you act rather than lapse into paralysis. Frames give you strategies for responding to surprising and stressful situations that would otherwise be overwhelming.

Both your pre-service and in-service training provided many ideas and concepts to help you understand individual students, teaching methods, and curriculum. But teachers are almost never provided with lenses to help them understand the nature of leadership and the complex systems in which leadership is exercised. What they don't teach in teacher education is how to broaden your vision, how to sense the deeper social dynamics in your classroom and your school, and how to work with others to transform schools from the isolating and underrewarding environments that they so often become.

Much of our work has been with people in so-called "leadership positions"—the administrative and managerial roles that exist in every kind of institution and organization around the world. On the basis of our work with administrators and executives, we have found that they are more successful when they learn to use multiple frames, each offering a different angle on the challenges of leadership. The ability to use multiple frames has three advantages: (1) each frame can be coherent, focused, and powerful; (2) the collection can be more comprehensive than any single frame; and (3) only when you have multiple frames can you *reframe.* Reframing is a conscious effort to size up a situation from multiple perspectives. In times of crisis and overload, you will almost inevitably feel confused and overwhelmed if you are stuck with only one way to look at things. Think about dealing with a particularly difficult student. Sometimes, when you get trapped in the wrong approach, you are immobilized, and the student controls the situation. Other times, you may plunge mindlessly forward into reckless and misguided action. You fly off the handle and make things worse by escalating the conflict. When we don't know what to do, we often do more of what we know, even if it makes things worse instead of better.

We have identified four frames that are in common use among teachers as well as administrators:

1. The *human resource* frame is a favorite among teachers. It highlights the importance of needs and motives. It holds that classrooms, like other social systems, work best when individual needs are satisfied in a caring, trusting work environment. Showing concern for others and providing ample opportunities for participation and shared decision making are among the ways to enlist people's commitment and involvement. Many teachers have found that involving students in formulating classroom procedures and having them help in shaping instructional approaches gives them a sense of ownership in what happens each day.

2. The *political frame* points out the limits of authority and the inevitability that resources are too scarce to fulfill all demands.

Schools and classrooms are arenas where individuals and groups jockey for power. Teachers and students are both caught up in this swirling vortex of political activity. Goals emerge from bargaining and compromise among different interests rather than from rational analysis at the top. Conflict becomes an inescapable, even welcomed, by-product of everyday life. Handled properly, it is a source of constant energy and renewal.

3. The *structural frame* emphasizes productivity and assumes that classrooms and schools work best when goals and roles are clear, and when the efforts of individuals and groups are well coordinated through authority, policies, and rules, as well as through more informal strategies.

4. The *symbolic frame* centers attention on symbols, meaning, belief, and faith. Every classroom, like every human group, creates symbols to cultivate commitment, hope, and loyalty. Symbols govern behavior through informal, implicit, and shared rules, agreements, and understandings. Stories, metaphors, heroes and heroines, ritual, ceremony, and play add zest and existential buoyancy. The school becomes a way of life rather than merely a place of work.

In dealing with classroom challenges, most teachers rely primarily on the human resource or structural lenses. Yet many of the situations you face contain highly charged symbolic challenges that are politically and emotionally powerful. That people are young does not diminish their ability to use power to get their way, nor lessen their need for symbols to provide meaning and hope. The classroom is a jungle and a cathedral as much as it is a family or a production system. If you sometimes feel that each day brings another series of ambushes and pitfalls, reframing can help. It can also help in dealing with schoolwide issues or situations that difficult parents or district-office intrusion can present.

In our teaching and consulting, we have presented the idea of reframing to thousands of professionals around the world. As they learn to understand and apply the frames, they regularly tell us three things:

1. The frames stay with them because they are easy to remember.

2. The frames help them see things they did not notice before and help them understand what is really going on.

3. When they are able to reframe, people see new possibilities and become more versatile and effective in their responses.

We think these same lessons apply to the world of the classroom teacher. The book is designed as a portable mentor. Through a close and intense dialogue between a new teacher and a seasoned veteran, the novice comes to see troublesome situations more clearly, to anticipate trouble before it arises, and to develop more comprehensive and powerful strategies for leadership. We believe that the challenges facing other teachers are similar to those encountered by the new teacher who is the protagonist for this book, Joan Hilliard. Sometimes, the outcomes that Joan achieves may seem remarkably upbeat and positive compared to similar situations that you have witnessed. We deliberately made Joan a highly committed and talented young teacher who persists in the face of obstacles and who learns from her mistakes. She is also blessed with some very helpful colleagues (as well as a few not so helpful ones). We have all read plenty of accounts of what's wrong with schools. We want to provide a more optimistic view—a hopeful image of the possibilities for teacher leadership.

Chapter 1, "A New Teacher's First Day," takes a new teacher, Joan Hilliard, through her first exciting but puzzling day at work. In Chapter 2, "Realities Burst the Bubble," Joan Hilliard's initial excitement turns to dismay in the face of challenges both in the classroom and at home. She struggles with how to deal with Roscoe, a mischievous student. At the same time, Larry, her longtime boyfriend, is finding it hard to understand why Joan is bringing so much work home with her every evening. Fortunately, a wise veteran, Margaret Juhl, volunteers to help out. The four subsequent chapters are each built around a specific challenge that Hilliard encounters in her early months as a teacher. For each problem, Margaret Juhl uses ideas from one of the frames to help Joan get a better handle on what is happening and what to do about it.

In Chapter 3, "Building Effective Relationships: The Human Resource View," Hilliard struggles with relationships in several directions: (1) with Roscoe, the most mischievous boy in her class; (2) with Larry, who can't seem to understand why Joan's first year as a teacher is demanding so much of her time; and (3) with the new principal, Jaime Rodriguez. Basic ideas from the human resource frame help Joan see new possibilities for building more effective relationships.

In Chapter 4, "The Tracking Wars: Dealing With School Politics," Joan and a group of her colleagues become enthusiastic about enhancing Pico School's commitment to the district's new inclusion policy, but they are dismayed at the resistance they encounter from other teachers. Margaret explains the sources of political dynamics in schools and shows Joan how to map those dynamics so as to be more effective in responding to them.

Chapter 5, "Student Discipline: Understanding Structure in Schools," explores the sometimes-neglected issues of the structural frame. Joan takes a leadership role in an effort to revise the school's discipline policy, but becomes frustrated when the process seems hopelessly bogged down. Juhl helps Hilliard see that the process for revising the policy was unintentionally designed for failure. After the process is redesigned to clarify goals, roles, and accountability, the school is finally able to develop a policy that works. In the same chapter, Margaret also gives Joan a lesson in "upward leadership": how to lead your principal so that she or he can better lead the school.

In Chapter 6, " 'I'm Just a Great Teacher': Using Symbols to Revive the Spirit," Joan is struck to find that many of the veteran teachers in her school seem to have lost some of the spark and spirit that brought them to teaching in the first place. They lament the years of low pay, lack of respect, and bureaucratic frustrations. But they come to realize that, at a more profound level, they face a crisis of meaning and faith. They become energized by the process of developing a celebration of teaching as an opening event for the fall term, and the celebration becomes a transforming experience for Pico's teaching staff.

The next two chapters show how all four frames can be applied to the same issue. In Chapter 7, "Teaching and Leading: Balancing Family and Career," levels of energy and commitment at Pico have reached a new high, but the breakup of Joan's and Larry's relationship is the catalyst for a schoolwide discussion of how educators can learn to balance commitments to career, family, and private life.

Chapter 8, "The Essence of Teaching: Leaving a Legacy," begins when tragedy enters Margaret Juhl's life as she is stricken with breast cancer. The entire Pico community rallies around her, and this bout with mortality leads Margaret and Joan into a dialogue about the purposes and values underlying teaching as a profession.

In Chapter 9, "The Torch is Passed," Joan Hilliard confronts tragedy and loss, looks deep within herself, and finds the inner strength to rededicate herself to her calling.

"Epilogue: Diagnosis and Action," provides a brief overview of the major ideas Juhl and Hilliard discussed in earlier chapters.

The dialogue between Joan Hilliard and Margaret Juhl is much like those that we have with educational leaders all the time. Our role is usually to offer questions more than answers. When the questions are chosen well, they help people see things in new ways and recognize promising leadership opportunities that were there all along. When school leaders are able to reframe situations, they become more confident and more certain. They feel less anxious and overwhelmed. Most important, they are more effective and get more done.

We hope you will find the conversation between Hilliard and Juhl both lively and informative. We grounded the book in the real world of schools and in the experiences of practicing teachers. The book offers a return to an old-fashioned approach to learning a craft. Joan Hilliard and Margaret Juhl do not have all the answers to the mysteries of school leadership, but they are concerned about many of the same questions and issues that are important to you. You will find yourself almost automatically applying new perspectives and insights to the challenges you face in your own job. We hope that their conversation will stimulate you to think more deeply about yourself and your approach to leadership. Teachers are among the most important leaders in America. Ask a random sample of adults to name the most important leader they have known personally. Many will immediately talk about a caring and gifted teacher who inspired them in a life-changing way. Above all, we hope the book will help you find new paths to confidence and success—and deepen your contribution to the students and others who count on you for leadership.

A New Teacher's First Day

Joan Hilliard could feel the smile on her face as she stepped out of her car. It was not the best vehicle in the world, but it was hers, one of the benefits of her four years working for a large brokerage firm. In college Joan had majored in education because she had always wanted to be a teacher. To her great disappointment, when she graduated there were no teaching positions to be found anywhere near where she wanted to live. She had been determined to teach eventually but decided that any job was better than nothing, and the brokerage firm paid well. Now, she was finally going to have her own classroom. She even felt she was better off with four years of experience. She had learned a lot about herself, about working with others, and about organizational life, and she had a more realistic appraisal of the costs and benefits of being in the private sector. Above all, she felt more confident. She had learned how to cope in a demanding and stressful environment, a skill she was sure would stand her in good stead in the classroom.

She was delighted to get an assignment to Pico, a school with one of the best reputations in the area. It looked like a friendly place from the outside. The surrounding neighborhood had declined from its earlier glory, but the school had green lawns, well-trimmed shrubbery, and lots of large, lattice-paned windows. Built in the 1940s, the school had much of the architectural charm that Joan remembered in the schools of her childhood. As she walked through the arched entry way, Joan noticed the familiar smell of a school just before the students arrive in the fall. "Probably a blend of new wax on the floors and mustiness from the summer," she thought to herself. As she turned down the corridor leading to the principal's office, she noticed a tall, broad-shouldered man with his hands on his hips, studying carefully the sheen on the floor. Joan wondered if this was the custodian admiring his work before thousands of student feet obscured it with a mosaic of scuff marks.

As Joan moved closer, the man looked up at her with a smile as if he had expected her. "You must be Joan Hilliard, the new teacher. I'm Bill Hill, the chief custodian. Let me know if I can help you get settled. I'll stop by occasionally to see how you're doing and let you know what's going on."

"Is this the way to the principal's office?" asked Joan, slightly puzzled about what kind of news the custodian planned to bring her.

"Straight ahead, second door on the left," Hill replied. "I hear you used to work at a brokerage firm. Not as fancy here. You'll probably find you even have to buy some of your own supplies. Of course, our kids are a lot different from the adults that you've been working with. They need a lot of discipline, but a lot of caring, too. My own philosophy is that. . . ."

"Thank you very much, Mr. Hill. I'm sorry I can't chat longer, but I don't want to be late for my meeting with Mr. Rodriguez."

"Oh, don't worry, he's new too. I hope he's as good as our old principal, Mr. Bailey. We worked together for years. He was a wonderful man. Anyway, you run along. We'll have plenty of time to talk later. I'll drop by your room after lunch. It's good to see a new player on the team."

Joan continued down the hall, all the while trying to make sense out of her encounter with Bill Hill. "He almost sounds as if he runs the place. He'll probably read what I put on the board before he erases it. At Barker and Lloyd's the custodians never volunteered their ideas about how the market was doing."

As she opened the glass door labeled "Principal's Office," Joan's reverie was interrupted by a cheerful voice. "Yoo hoo, Ms. Hilliard, welcome to Pico!" The voice belonged to a smiling gray-haired woman wearing a "Pico Pride" t-shirt over a pair of blue jeans. "I'm Phyllis Gleason, the school secretary. Mr. Rodriguez got called to the superintendent's office unexpectedly. He'll fill you in on the school and your assignment when he gets back. In the meantime, he asked me to show you around. Would you like a cup of coffee before we start?"

"Sure, why not?"

As Phyllis went off in search of coffee, the door to an office marked "Assistant Principal" opened, and a short, square-shouldered, graying man walked out. He looked at Joan, frowned and asked, "Who are you?"

His tone and his crew-cut both reminded Joan of a drill sergeant, and she was surprised at how nervous she felt. "Oh, uh, I'm sorry. I'm Joan Hilliard, and I . . ."

"Oh, yeah!" the man interrupted, with the commanding tone of someone who expected to be listened to. "I heard about you. It's bad enough you don't have any teaching experience, but I know you didn't learn anything about classroom control from a bunch of stockbrokers. Some of those guys don't even know anything about the market, much less about handling kids." With that, he marched forcefully out of the office just as Phyllis returned with the coffee.

Phyllis seemed to understand immediately what Joan was feeling. "Oh, you met Mr. Shepherd. Well, don't take it personally. I'm not sure if his bark is worse than his bite, but he's the same with everyone."

"I didn't exactly meet him," Joan replied. "He didn't bother to tell me who he was. Is he the assistant principal?"

"Oh yes, Sam Shepherd, he's been assistant principal here for ten years. Some people even thought he might become the next principal. But maybe the superintendent felt that Mr. Shepherd should do what he does best. He's *awfully* strong on discipline."

Joan was not sure whether Phyllis intended to communicate praise or veiled criticism of the assistant principal, so she decided not to press the issue. She felt disappointed that Rodriguez was not there, and wondered if a tour led by the school secretary would simply be a time-filler. But her doubts turned to awe and admiration as Gleason led her through the building. Phyllis seemed to know everything about Pico and recounted it in loving detail as if she had witnessed it all firsthand. Gleason introduced Joan with unflagging enthusiasm to everyone they encountered on their tour, and Joan was impressed with the warmth of the responses. Joan was even more amazed with Gleason's ability to field questions on just about everything—schedules, materials, children, and parents.

"They treat her like the school oracle—knows all, tells all, whatever she says is the way it is," thought Joan thought to herself. "It sure seems as if Phyllis is the person to know around here." It was only as they neared the end of the tour that Joan also realized how much of her own background and ideas about teaching she had shared with Phyllis. "She seems as interested in how I think about teaching as Bill Hill did," mused Joan.

Phyllis stopped in front of a door with an opaque window marked 208. She took Joan inside a small, well-worn classroom and said, "This is your room this year. What do you think? Maybe it's a little plain compared to what you're used to. But at least within these four walls, you're the boss."

"It's great! Lots of windows, plenty of wall space and book shelves. The walls are a little bare, but we'll take care of that in no time." Joan's mind was flooded with a thousand thoughts. It seemed as if she had been waiting forever for this moment. She tried to imagine the empty desks filled with students. Her students. Her classroom.

Phyllis waited for a few moments while Joan took it all in. "I'll leave you alone for a while to think about what else you'll need. Whatever it is, I'll try to get it for you. Maybe I should mention one thing. The teacher that you're replacing left us after last year. He was very smart, but he wasn't able to control his class. He was here for a couple of years, but never quite seemed to fit in. I know you'll be different. And, anything you need to know, come to me." Phyllis smiled once again and started back to the principal's office, turning her head only to acknowledge Joan's thank you.

After her rescheduled meeting with Jaime Rodriguez, Joan mulled over her morning's encounters. It was not what she had expected. She was particularly curious about why the secretary and the custodian seemed to be so important and so much involved in what classroom teachers did. She felt apprehension as she wondered just how many people might be looking over her shoulder and giving her advice on how to teach. She did not quite feel comfortable enough to raise concerns with Mr. Rodriguez, even though he seemed very friendly and genuinely pleased that she was joining the Pico faculty. They had formed an almost instant bond as they talked about the fact that both of them were new to Pico and both felt a little scared about how things would go. She could hardly believe her luck in finding a principal who seemed so supportive and easy to work with.

The day's thoughts were still spinning in Joan's mind as she walked to her car for the drive home. Just as she was opening the front door of her car, she heard someone calling her name. She turned her head and saw a group of teachers chatting in the parking lot. One of them came over. "Joan Hilliard?" he said as he offered his hand. "I'm Phil Leckney, and my classroom is just down the hall from yours. Welcome to Pico. A couple of us are headed over to Andy's Cafe. Would you like to join us?"

Joan felt torn. She had promised her boyfriend Larry that she would meet him at 4:30 and it was 4:00 already. After hesitating, she replied, "Well, I can only stay for a little while, but I'd love to."

The conversation at Andy's reinforced Joan's feeling that she had made the right decision in taking a job at Pico. Even though she got the impression that Leckney probably had not learned anything new about teaching in at least 20 years, she liked everyone she met. She was especially impressed with Margaret Juhl. Juhl was Pico's representative for the teachers union and, Joan quickly realized, one of the most respected teachers at Pico. When Joan told of her encounters with Bill Hill and Phyllis Gleason, her new colleagues laughed heartily.

"To understand Bill," said Margaret, "all you have to do is come in some morning at 7:30 and go to the cafeteria where the 'free breakfast' kids are eating. Bill is always there, and you'll see he's like a big brother to just about everyone in the room. Not only that, he knows a lot of their parents too. He grew up around here and he probably knows more people in the community than anyone else at Pico."

"Well, it might be a tie between him and Phyllis. She's sort of a combination of Dear Abby, Diane Sawyer, and General Patton. The key thing you gotta remember is the line from the old song, 'You can get anything you want, at Phyllis's restaurant.' "

Joan joined everyone else's laughter. As the group quieted down, Joan was surprised by a question from Vivian Chu. Chu, another veteran, had not said much until she turned to Joan and said, "You met with Mr. Rodriguez this morning, didn't you? How did the meeting go?" It became clear to her that her colleagues were as curious as she was about Pico's new principal.

As Phil Leckney put it, "He's an unknown quantity. Phil Bailey was a great guy. Not Mr. Superprincipal, maybe, but he was pretty supportive, and he let us teach. Is this guy going to understand how we do things around here? How hard is it going to be to break him in?"

No one seemed to know the answer. The consensus was that they would need to wait until the school's first faculty meeting to get a better sense. Then the conversation shifted to Joan's experience in the business world. Her colleagues peppered her with questions about what she did, what it was like, and, to her embarrassment, how much money she had made. It almost felt as if they wished they had tasted another career themselves to find out if the grass was greener somewhere else. The conversation at Andy's was so engrossing that Joan was startled to look at her watch and notice that she was half an hour late for her meeting with Larry. Bidding her colleagues a hasty farewell, she rushed off. On balance, she felt, it had been a great day. She just hoped that Larry was not too miffed that she was late.

Realities Burst the Bubble

There could not have been a worse day for Roscoe to act out. As usual, he had managed to draw Armando into his latest mischief designed to ruin a teacher's afternoon. Joan had tried just about everything short of wringing both of their necks, with little success. Nothing she had learned in college or business had prepared her for this. What was usually a productive well-organized classroom had turned into a dreadful mess that felt like a combination of a zoo and Beirut on a bad day for each.

Joan felt exasperated. She wondered if she would have enough energy to finish planning tomorrow's lessons and then meet Larry for dinner in the evening. She was only a few days into the term, and school was already spilling over too often into their relationship. When it did, evenings became one more vexing challenge instead of a warm and welcome escape. In her previous job, the work day started early but always ended in time for dinner, and she almost never had to take work home with her. As she asked herself whether she was more in need of an after-school glass of wine or fifteen minutes on a Stairmaster, Joan was heartened when Margaret Juhl walked into her classroom and offered Joan's first adult hello of the day.

"Rough day?" asked Margaret.

"Worse than that," replied Joan. "I've been through one of Roscoe's romps—with accompaniment from Armando. They literally destroyed this afternoon. I always believed in inclusion until Roscoe came along. He's the worst example of displaced energy I have ever seen. Nothing works. When he loses it, he's simply uncontrollable. It's been hell! I figured kids couldn't be that much tougher than some of the adults I worked with. But an angry client or a pompous broker is a lot easier than this."

Margaret smiled. "I get at least one child like that just about every year. Deep down, you love them, but they can drive you nuts. When you get through to them, you feel wonderful. But when you can't, it breaks your heart. In the meantime, you've got to keep ahead of it. If you get behind, you have a year of misery ahead of you."

"Well, it's my first year, and I'm afraid I'm already behind," responded Joan with a dejected look. "What makes it even harder is that Roscoe is a natural leader. When he goes off the deep end, the rest of the lemmings are right behind. And Armando thinks that he's Sancho Panza, following his master to the end."

"Well, if it's any comfort, my nemesis this year is Wanda. She's about the same size as Roscoe, and may have even more energy. Figuring out how to handle her has kept me up a few nights."

"But, Margaret," interjected Joan, "you've got the best rep of any teacher in this school. With the number of years you've got under your belt I thought all this would be a cinch."

"In teaching, there are no cinches. Experience helps you put things in perspective, but each year brings a new set of Wandas, Roscoes, Armandos, and Lucies. Lucy is Wanda's coconspirator. Your training never really prepares you for it."

"Well, it sure helps just knowing that I'm not alone," said Joan with a smile. "Everything has been feeling so overwhelming and so stressful, I'm beginning to wonder if I'll ever make it through the year."

"The headaches never go away completely. The heartaches don't either. But in time, they become part of what teaching is all about. You just have to put them in perspective. Good teachers learn how to do it. Just between us chickens, some people never do. They either get out or burn out. You remind me a little bit of me. I can remember a similar tussle 25 years ago with a little boy named Jimmy who was in the first class I ever taught. He always looked angelic, but on the first day of school, he cursed during the pledge of allegiance. I didn't know what to do, and it got worse from there. For a while I started to feel that he had more control over me than I had over the class. Roscoe sounds a lot like Jimmy. There's a Spanish word for them: *picaro*. It means the face of an angel and the soul of the devil."

"What did you do about Jimmy?" asked Joan.

"I got lucky. Dorothy Runyon came into my life about the same time that I seem to be coming into yours. She was an amazing lady, and she knew more about teaching than I ever hope to know. I learned a lot from her, and some of it might even help you with Roscoe. I'm always glad for an opportunity to pay back some of the help I got from her."

"I can't believe it," said Joan. "Everyone says that the first year of teaching is a lot like being tossed into a swimming pool. You pretty much sink or swim on your own. I didn't have much hope for a life vest just down the hall, but I sure need one. Maybe I shouldn't even ask this, but do you also give advice on love life?"

Joan hesitated until she saw Margaret smile warmly. Then she continued, "I've been going with a guy named Larry ever since I was in college, and things were fine until I started teaching. He can't understand what the job is like and why I never seem to have much time for him anymore. I know he's about ready to tell me that either Pico goes or he goes. How do I convince him that things are going to get better? In fact, I'm supposed to meet him for dinner in an hour and I've got a million things left to do."

Margaret laughed gently. "Well, I'm not sure I'm much of an expert on how to deal with Larry. My life is wonderful, but it's like a modern version of the old school marm. I'm single, but I have fun and I have a full life away from the school. I'll tell you what. Let me meet this Larry and see if I have any ideas after I get to know him. Why don't you finish up what you're working on, and then we'll both go meet Larry. Maybe a one-two punch might help him see the light."

Building Effective Relationships:
The Human Resource View

So when are you going to be through today?"
Joan was surprised by the harsh tone of Larry's question. He was still in bed, and she was just finishing the final touches on her teaching costume for the day. The night before had been wonderful. Larry seemed genuinely captivated by Margaret's stories. It was almost as if he could also feel a little of the magic of teaching at its best. Each time Margaret had told a story about a student, Larry had responded with a tale about a teacher who had meant something to him. Before they went to sleep, Larry had given her the supreme compliment: "Honey, I may be out to make a fortune, but in your new career you're destined to make a difference." But now, in the light of day, he seemed to be back to his usual, unsympathetic self.

"I'm not sure, Larry," she said carefully. "Today is the day that Margaret and I are meeting with the principal to talk about his opening sermon. You remember, I told you about it."

"Oh, yeah. That's when Rodriguez gave his vision thing, and Margaret cut him off at the knees."

"Well, not quite," said Joan, as she thought back to the first faculty meeting of the new school year. She remembered the meeting vividly. Joan had felt an instant bond when she first met Pico's principal, Jaime Rodriguez. Both of them were brand-new—both to the school and to their positions. Jaime seemed to feel the same mix of excitement and apprehension about his first principalship that Joan was feeling about her first teaching assignment.

Joan knew that Rodriguez wanted to get off on the right foot as much as she did. She had entered the first faculty meeting with optimism and excitement. After a few preliminaries, Rodriguez started to speak about his vision for the school. Joan felt initially excited about his image of a child-centered school in which all students were expected to succeed and to achieve at their full potential. In her previous job, there never seemed to be any real sense of mission beyond making more money.

Even though Rodriguez seemed tense, he delivered his message with conviction, even fervor. As he spoke, Joan began to notice that many teachers seemed not to share her excitement. Some seemed openly resistant or disinterested. A few sat with their arms crossed. Others were simply staring out the window or glancing at papers in front of them. When Rodriguez finished, he asked for questions. At first, none came. The silence was oppressive, and Joan could not remember when she had felt more tension in a room. Everyone just sat in stony silence until Margaret Juhl asked, "Shouldn't you get to know this school and how we do things before you tell us how to teach?"

Joan was startled by Margaret's bluntness and was pained when she glanced at Jaime Rodriguez. He looked stunned, almost frozen in place. Joan wished she had the courage to go over and give him a hug. "He looks like he needs help," she thought to herself in the seconds before another young teacher, Carlos Cortez, leapt to his feet and spoke with obvious anger in his voice.

"The man just got here, and you people don't even want to give him a chance. Mr. Rodriguez is saying things that someone has needed to say for a long time. I'm getting pretty tired of people who think this school is so perfect that we can't change anything." Cortez's outburst triggered a series of sharply worded exchanges among older and younger teachers. Joan began to wonder what she had gotten herself into. She had never seen anything like this in her old firm. The climate there had been competitive, even cutthroat, but people never shouted at one another. She felt horrible and was relieved when Rodriguez moved quickly to adjourn the meeting.

Joan continued to think back to that meeting as she went to the kitchen to get another cup of coffee before leaving for school. Equally vivid in her mind was a conversation after the meeting when she asked Margaret to explain what had happened.

"Well," said Juhl, "I'm still sorting it out myself. Jaime is probably feeling a little shell-shocked, wondering what hit him. And he may be pretty angry at me."

"Aren't you worried about that?" Joan asked.

"Only if he stays angry. He could make life difficult for me if he wanted to," Margaret replied.

"Do you think maybe you should apologize to him, or something?" Joan asked.

"Of course not. He may not know it yet," said Margaret with a smile, "but I was doing him a favor."

"A kick in the teeth is a favor?" asked Joan in obvious disbelief.

"You were there, and you saw all those stony faces. He meant well, but his speech flopped with most of the faculty, and he didn't have a clue about what was going wrong. It may take a little while, but he might realize that I was actually telling him just what he needed to know: why the teachers didn't like his opening salvo."

"But, what if he doesn't?" asked Joan.

"We'll know tomorrow," answered Margaret. "He called and asked if we could meet."

"Carlos was fuming, too," said Joan. "Are you going to wait for him to get to you, too?"

"No, I'll go to Carlos. Right now, he may think I'm leading a conservative charge to undermine the district's first Hispanic principal. The truth is, I want Jaime to succeed as much as Carlos does. If a teacher really wants to torpedo an administrator, you don't do it with a frontal assault. You do them in with silent resistance and passive aggression. You probably saw the same thing in your last job. Rodriguez was digging himself into a hole. I wanted him to be aware of what he was doing and remind him about the first law of holes."

"The first law of holes?"

"When you're in one, stop digging!" said Margaret with a laugh. "Anyway, if I take the initiative to talk to Carlos one-on-one about how we can work together to help the new principal succeed, I think we can have a meeting of the minds."

"I don't know," said Joan skeptically. "He seemed pretty upset."

"Joan, when I was younger, I used to pussyfoot around disagreement and conflict. I was afraid of getting people angry or upset. But I slowly realized I was just sweeping things under the rug until the lumps got so big we tripped over them. Teaching is not an exact science, and we're not always going to agree with one another. And if we're at loggerheads about things we all care about, how in the world can we deal with our disagreements if we don't talk about them?"

"Maybe that's why everyone's pussyfooting around the tensions between the Latino and Anglo teachers?" asked Joan.

"Exactly. People are hoping that if we ignore it it will go away. But we know it won't, and in the meantime we hurt the kids as much as we hurt each other. The same thing happens with all the other conflicts we try to brush aside. They pile up and either smoulder or blow up. That's not my idea of a healthy school. It's like the old saying that you can't make an omelette without breaking any eggs. In the long run, it's more productive and more fun to get things out in the open."

"Just the same, you really left Jaime hanging out," said Joan. "He looked crushed after you went after him."

"I know—it was painful for both of us. But the one thing worse than hearing something straight is getting no feedback at all. If you looked around the room, you saw crossed arms and people rolling their eyes. It wasn't even subtle. There were a lot of unhappy teachers in that audience. The problem is that a lot of times real feelings never come out in the open. So teachers can think their new principal is a jerk, but he doesn't know it. Down the road, he notices that the teachers seem to be resisting everything he's doing to improve the school. So he figures that the teachers are rigid, or unmotivated, or dinosaurs—or whatever."

"So everyone blames someone else, and the school gets stuck. But, then, why did you convene the meeting at Andy's cafe without Jaime? Weren't you being less than open yourself?" asked Joan.

"In the short run, maybe. But I knew teachers were going to be talking about what happened. I knew what I said to Jaime would be seen as a message from a lot of people, not just from me. You remember how the conversation at Andy's went. After our colleagues got a chance to vent their rage, you could see some of them starting to feel sympathy for Jaime. By the time people left Andy's that night, they were a little more willing to at least give him another chance. That's just what I hoped the meeting would do."

"But you still hurt his feelings," said Joan. "I really felt bad for him. He's new in his job, just like me. I don't know if I could take anyone picking me apart like that in public. It's bad enough that Larry has already given me more criticism than I ever wanted about my cooking, but right now, I'm feeling so vulnerable about my teaching. If you told me what I was doing wrong with Roscoe in front of everyone, I'm not sure I could take it."

Margaret's face softened. Her voice was warm and gentle. "I know, and I know that Jaime is probably feeling pretty vulnerable, too. I remember how much support I needed when I was a new teacher. But I also needed people to level with me when I was doing things that weren't working. Would you want Larry to keep you in the dark, so you could keep feeding him stuff he hates? If I came up with any ideas for what you could do differently with Roscoe, would you want to hear them?"

"If you can help with Roscoe, even public humiliation might not be too big a price to pay. But it still wouldn't feel very good to me, and I don't think Jaime is feeling so hot either. He's probably still pretty upset."

"Sure, he is. Building an open relationship takes more than just firing a salvo and leaving the person high and dry. You have to follow up. That's what I'm planning to do tomorrow. Would you like to come along?"

"I don't know. Are you sure you want me to?"

"Sure. With your business experience, you might have something to contribute, and you can give me some feedback. Pico is my professional life, and I want Jaime to be successful. What I said in the meeting might have looked like a hatchet job—to both you and Jaime. The meeting tomorrow is a chance to clear the air."

As Joan took her last sip of coffee, her long reverie was interrupted by Larry's insistent words, "Earth to Hilliard! Earth to

Hilliard! Are you still there? You've been staring at the coffee pot for the last five minutes. I thought you were going to bring me a cup."

"I'm sorry, honey. I guess I was still thinking about yesterday. Anyway, I'm sure the meeting today can't last beyond 5:00. How about pizza? My treat?"

"Sounds great, *if* you promise not to get pizza topped with pepperoni *and* Pico."

"I promise," said Joan laughing. There were still moments when Larry was as delightful as she remembered him in graduate school. But he had seemed much more supportive of her career when they were both in the same business. Now that she was teaching, he seemed to expect that *her* work day should last from the time *he* left in the morning until *he* got home at night. Even though he seemed to understand a little more after the conversation with Margaret, Joan wondered if they would ever make it over the long haul.

That afternoon in Jaime's office, Joan finally saw what Margaret had been trying to say. She was impressed when Margaret opened the meeting by asking Jaime to share some of his feelings about the incident. She was particularly struck with Margaret's ability to be supportive, warm, and confronting all at the same time. But the warmest spot for her came when she observed the final exchange between the two.

"I guess I was so anxious about getting established and giving the school a vision," said Jaime, "that I lost track of the teachers' feelings. I know Pico has a lot of experienced teachers who feel they're doing a good job and have a lot of excellent ideas of their own. I didn't say that and I should have. I'll admit, I didn't like your comment at the time. In fact I was floored. But, in a way, you were just giving me a dose of what I was giving the teachers."

"Do you also understand I wasn't trying to make you look bad," said Margaret, "but to give you a clear warning that you were about to drive over a cliff?"

"That's clearer to me now than it was then. And it's also getting pretty obvious that I'm a lot better off with teachers who are willing to tell me the truth than those who pretend to be satisfied and then talk behind my back, or stick it to me when I'm not looking. Thanks, Margaret. I'll tell you, I never expected this kind of conversation with the teachers' union rep."

"Well, that's not the hat I'm wearing right now. We can be colleagues about a lot of things, and I believe in looking for a cooperative relationship wherever it's possible. I *will* fight as hard as necessary to represent the teachers when I'm wearing my union rep hat. In either case, I'll be straight with you."

Joan thought about the conversation between Jaime and Margaret all the way to the Pizza Pad. If she had not been so late getting there, Larry might have been more receptive when she tried to explain how much she had learned. She was taken aback when he grumbled, "First of all you're late. Second, you promised this morning I wouldn't have to have Pico with my pizza. Now you ruin what could be a very romantic evening by breaking your promise. Frankly, I'm getting fed up!"

Joan wanted to respond, but found nothing to say as the tears streamed down her cheeks. She felt embarrassed, guilty, and angry all at the same time. "He's right," she thought to herself, "I did break my promise. But if Larry cared a little more about me and a little less about himself, the relationship might work a lot better." She resisted the temptation to tell him that she wished his father had coached him as much on building relationships as on getting ahead. Recognizing the impulse to hurl accusations back at him, she asked herself what Margaret would do. Instead of firing back, she tried to draw Larry out. "Do you feel like I'm putting Pico ahead of you?"

"That's an understatement if I ever heard one."

"You remember what it was like a few years ago when we were both starting out at Barker and Lloyd's?"

"Well, I know things were hectic, and we were both very busy. But I didn't burden you with every problem that came up at work."

"Did you ever ask me how I felt?" Joan asked.

Larry glanced sheepishly down at his slice of pizza. "Well, I figured you'd tell me if you were bothered by anything."

"That's why I'm asking you now. How I felt then is exactly what you're feeling now. I didn't say much because I figured you had enough to worry about. But I'm learning that we really have to talk to each other to make this relationship work."

Larry laughed amiably. "You're turning into a 24-hour teacher."

"I hope not," said Joan with a smile, "and I promise, no more Pico with the pizza."

The next morning Joan burst excitedly into Margaret Juhl's classroom before school began. "You're not going to believe this, but watching you talk to Jaime helped me deal with Larry last night. I'm not sure exactly what happened, but it worked."

Margaret asked Joan to review the conversation of the previous evening. Then she said, "I think I have an idea about why it worked. It sounds like each of you had needs that the other wasn't responding to very well, partly because you hadn't really talked about them. You needed Larry to understand the pressures you're feeling in your first year of teaching. He needed you to understand how frustrated he gets when it seems you can never leave your job behind.

"It's kind of amazing how often we keep each other in the dark and then get frustrated when people don't read our minds. Someone once called it the mystery-mastery model. When there's a problem, we blame it on someone else. Then we develop our own private strategy to get the other person to change. We pressure them, manipulate them, and tell them what they're doing wrong. A lot of times it doesn't work very well, but when they resist, we blame them for not listening, for being defensive. We know they should improve, but if they don't, it's not our fault, because we did our best."

Joan was squirming, because everything Margaret was saying struck all too close to her relationship with Larry. "So what's the alternative?"

"Cooperation and communication. For example, basically you have to build your relationship with Larry around the things that you have in common. Like, you want him to care about you, and he wants you to care about him. If you can say that, you can talk about how to meet each other's needs."

"Of course!" said Joan with excitement. "Instead of really being honest about what I want from Larry, I've been criticizing him for not giving it to me. And he's doing it to me. What's crazy is that we're at war when we both feel pretty much the same thing."

"It happens all the time," replied Margaret, "because we forget that a relationship is always a two-way street. You need to be open with Larry about what you need and what you're feeling, but you also need to test your assumptions and make sure you understand where he's coming from. When Larry said he was fed up last night, you could have told him he wasn't half as fed up as you were. Instead, you asked him if he felt you care more about the school than about him. You had a hunch about what he was feeling, and you checked it out. That's when the conversation really shifted, right?"

"Yeah. It's like instead of just blaming each other, we started talking about what was really going on between us." Joan thought for a moment, and then asked, "Do you think the same thing would work with Roscoe?"

"Give it a try," Margaret replied with a smile.

The Tracking Wars: Dealing With School Politics

Joan had some real doubts when Margaret first suggested trying to draw out Roscoe. "Still," she thought to herself, "nothing else is working, and this is probably worth a try." Roscoe and his side-kick Armando continued to make every day a struggle for control of the classroom. Nothing that she had learned in business seemed to be helping. It came to a head later that week when Joan received a first-hand account from Jaime Rodriguez of how Roscoe and Armando had man-handled the substitute while Joan was out for a day with the flu. The substitute had left after a public declaration that she would never take that class again. This troubled Rodriguez, because he had heard that this substitute could be counted on for last-minute assignments. Even though she was not surprised, Joan did not like Jaime Rodriguez's recommendation that she attend a conference on strategies for responding to exceptional youngsters. His suggestion made sense, but Joan felt like a failure. She agreed to go to the conference but decided to try in the meantime to de-velop her own home-grown strategy.

Her first step was to learn more about Roscoe from someone who knew him well, and she knew just the person to ask. Heidi

Hernandez was one of the brightest and most cooperative students in her class. Heidi was wise beyond her years, even though she tended to perform below the incredible potential that Joan saw in her. Heidi was the multitalented daughter of immigrant Venezuelan parents. She was usually happiest playing field hockey or dancing at her ballet class, but Joan was working hard to intrigue Heidi with the joys of schoolwork and learning as well. Heidi often stayed after school to talk to Joan about her own dream of going to college and becoming a teacher—even though no one else in her family had graduated from high school. Joan knew that Heidi and Roscoe lived in the same neighborhood, and, equally important, she knew she could trust Heidi.

As class was ending on a sunny Thursday afternoon, Joan struck up a conversation with Heidi. "You know Roscoe pretty well, don't you, Heidi?" she asked.

"Sure," said Heidi, "his house is right down the street from mine. Sometimes we walk to school together. It's good having someone to talk with. Sometimes, he's real nice. Other times, he's just plain mean."

"That's kind of how he is in class. Why do you think Roscoe gets mean sometimes?" asked Joan.

Heidi hesitated for a moment, and then asked for reassurance. "This won't get Roscoe in trouble, will it?"

"No, it won't," Joan replied, "I'm Roscoe's teacher as much as I am yours. Maybe you know something that would help me be a better teacher for him."

Heidi screwed up her face and thought for a moment about what Joan Hilliard had said. Then she appeared to relax and started to talk freely. "I think about him a lot, Miss Hilliard. I don't think Roscoe's mother takes very good care of him. She doesn't fix dinner for him the way my mom does for me. His father isn't home much, and when he's there he's really rough on him. He gets mad a lot, and he's always yelling at him. You may not know this, Miss Hilliard, but Roscoe's really happiest when he's at school. He thinks you're the best. I think he really wants you to like him, but he doesn't think he's smart enough. When he acts weird in class, at least he knows that he'll get your attention."

As she thanked Heidi, Joan tried hard not to show the emotion she was feeling. She already knew what she wanted to do next. The next day, she worried all day about how her meeting with Roscoe would turn out. As luck would have it, Roscoe was on reasonably good behavior all day. He seemed surprised when Joan asked him to stay for a while after the final bell had sounded.

"Come on, Miss Hilliard, what'd I do? Armando was the one that was causing all the trouble. Make him stay after school."

"You didn't do anything wrong," Joan assured him. "I just wanted to talk to you."

"About what?" asked Roscoe suspiciously.

"About you," said Joan.

Roscoe reluctantly agreed to stay. At first, he just stared at his feet, shifting his weight from leg to leg, with a sullen scowl on his face. He seemed afraid that Joan wanted to punish him for something. But as Joan began to ask how Roscoe felt about things, he sat down and looked up at her. He seemed to be looking for clues in Joan's expression. Then he started to talk in a low whisper, and Joan was surprised at what came out. He confirmed many of the things that Heidi had said a day earlier. He did not come right out and say it directly, but he hinted that Joan might be one of the reasons that he enjoyed coming to school. "You're pretty nice," he said. "My last teacher sent me to the office all the time. She said I was a pain. You don't do that, even when I'm bad."

"You know, I like you, Roscoe," Joan replied. "You're not really bad. You have a lot of spirit. It just does not always come out in the right ways. But let me ask you a question. Do you think you're doing as well as you could in school?"

Roscoe blushed and looked down at his scuffed shoes again. "I don't know," he said, "maybe not."

"Would you like to do better?" asked Joan.

He looked up, shrugged his shoulders, and said timidly, "I don't know if I can."

"I'm sure you can, and you just said so yourself. Maybe we could make a deal. I help you, and you help me. If we work together, you might be surprised at how well you do."

Roscoe smiled for the first time during their conversation. "You think so? O.K., Miss Hilliard, you've got yourself a deal." Then his expression changed to a look somewhere between earnest and impish. "But talk to Armando, too. He's the one who's always getting me in trouble."

As Roscoe left, Joan wondered how much she had gotten through to him. "Only time will tell," she thought, trying to be as optimistic as she could. Deep down, she was surprised at how much she was beginning to like Roscoe. As she drove home, she flashed back to the conversation. Some of Roscoe's expressions brought tears to her eyes. "Somehow, I'm going to get through to him. I've got to," she thought to herself.

The Monday morning after their conversation, Roscoe arrived in class with an apple for Joan. Even though it looked like a remnant from last season's crop, Joan was still exhilarated by the gesture. Even more gratifying was that Roscoe managed for one day to behave almost like an angel. Armando seemed so disappointed in the new Roscoe that he began to try to stir things up himself, but Roscoe simply told him, "Cut it out!"

Over the next few weeks, the results were mixed. Although Roscoe was not always true to his word, he did try—and he did improve. At times it seemed that he simply could not control himself. At other times, Joan could see him doing his best to resist the temptation to do something disruptive. But even when Roscoe was doing his best, Joan realized that he needed more help if he were to keep his promise for very long. At lunch one afternoon, she told Margaret what had happened with Roscoe over the last few weeks. "It's an improvement, but I still feel I need to do something more."

"Didn't Jaime offer to send you to that conference on classroom management? I went a few years ago. Even for someone who's been in the classroom a long time, I think it's pretty useful. It gave me some neat ideas for arranging the classroom differently that really help with all students, especially those with special needs. You might get some good ideas on ways to structure your classroom."

Margaret's endorsement was all Joan needed to tell Rodriguez that she was going to take his suggestion and attend the conference. She had anticipated that the biggest hurdle would be persuading Larry that it was worth her taking a weekend to go off to Platte University, and she dreaded one more harangue about being married to her work. The fates were kind for once, though—Larry had to be away on business the same weekend.

Joan almost flew to school the Monday morning after the conference. The program had been even better than she had expected. She had learned that she was not alone in her struggle to manage students like Roscoe, and she came away with at least a dozen ideas for things to do in her classroom. She also came away convinced that many of the issues went beyond her classroom and needed schoolwide changes in policies, such as rethinking the whole concept of student tracking. She was bubbling with enthusiasm when she turned in her expense report to Phyllis Gleason. Phyllis accepted the report with her usual cheerful efficiency but added an unexpected bit of cautionary advice:

"Joan," she said, "you look just as eager as some of the other teachers who've returned from conferences with a bag of new tricks. Just don't be disappointed if everyone isn't as excited about your new ideas as you are."

Carlos Cortez shared none of Phyllis's caution when Joan talked to him later that morning. Joan had expected Carlos to be supportive, and so she was thrilled that he seemed as excited about revising Pico's tracking system as she was. In fact, he quickly arranged for an informal afternoon meeting at Andy's Cafe with several other young teachers. Everyone there agreed that something needed to be done.

"We're labeling too many kids, shunting them off into special classes, or into classes for slower kids, and pretty much guaranteeing that they'll fall farther and farther behind. And it's particularly the minority kids who usually get labeled," said Carlos. "The district's new inclusion policy is a step in the right direction, but even though it was way overdue, there's still a lot of foot-dragging."

"What bothers me is that they're trying to be inclusive without giving teachers the support they need," Joan replied. "Here I am in my first year of teaching, and they gave me some very challenging kids without providing any help on what to do with them. I've been wondering, 'Why me?' It seems as if some of the older teachers figure out ways to get those students assigned to someone with less seniority."

"I've seen the same thing," replied Carlos. "What it means is that if you believe in inclusion, you wind up with all the special needs students that other teachers don't want. We really need everyone at Pico to get behind the inclusion policy and make it a schoolwide commitment. Otherwise, we're just creating a new form of tracking."

Everyone at the table agreed with Joan and Carlos. When they left Andy's later, they had all made a commitment to making the district's policy a part of Pico's philosophy and practice. Carlos and Joan went to work with enthusiasm to develop a presentation to Pico's faculty.

Their early optimism faded quickly during their presentation to the Pico faculty. They had talked to the principal, Jaime Rodriguez, beforehand and knew they had his support,. They expected questions and criticisms from some of their colleagues, but they were stunned by the outpouring of anger and resistance that swept over the meeting.

Phil Leckney, one of Pico's most senior teachers, led it off by questioning whether teachers with so little experience understood what they were getting into. "Look, guys," he said, "I've been to a lot of conferences, too. The eggheads in the universities always have some great new idea to save the world, but I've had a lot of years in the trenches. The folks with their heads in the clouds aren't talking reality because a lot of them have never taught in a public school classroom. They don't know what it's like."

Vivian Chu, always known as a staunch advocate of high academic standards, jumped in to support Leckney. "When we say that all children should learn, we sometimes wind up focusing all our attention on children who aren't learning, and forget those who are. The district has already cut funds for gifted and talented. Who's standing up for those kids? We have to provide a challenging education for our brightest kids. Not just for their benefit, but for everyone else's too. If we don't do the job, their parents will pull them out, and we'll lose kids who provide a model for everyone else. Then, there's all those kids in the middle. Sometimes they're the forgotten majority."

Leckney's and Chu's views received immediate support from a number of the veteran teachers. Even Margaret Juhl and Jaime

Rodriguez seemed powerless to turn back the tidal wave of staunch resistance to the proposal. The meeting ended in a stalemate, and a visibly shaken Joan grabbed Margaret on the way out of the room to ask in a trembling whisper if they could talk later. Margaret asked Joan to give her a call in the evening.

On the telephone that night, Joan got right to the point. "Could you believe that today? We're trying to help a lot of students who just aren't being served. A lot of those teachers are locked in concrete. They put their own convenience ahead of the needs of the kids."

Joan was surprised by Margaret's candid response. "I wish that you had talked to me before the meeting. A frontal assault like that usually invites a strong counterattack."

Joan was as surprised as she was disappointed. "What do you mean, 'frontal assault?' Whose side are you on, anyway?"

"Of course I'm on your side, because I think you're right," said Margaret, "but I understand where the others are coming from. This issue is not just about students. It has a lot to do with the same thing you're concerned about—managing differences. You remember how the battle lines were drawn between you and Roscoe earlier in the term. The standoff only began to change when you learned more about his side of things. You've got a similar situation here. But instead of a difference between two individuals, we now have a potential war between two groups with conflicting beliefs and interests. People are starting to rally the troops to make sure their interests triumph. When you have a political problem, you need a political strategy."

"This isn't about politics, it's about students. Why should I need a political strategy?" Joan asked skeptically.

"It may sound cynical, but it's also realistic. What's involved here is two groups with different beliefs who are struggling for what they think is right. Each group wants to win because they're sure their position is correct. The problem is that we'll all lose if we turn the school into a battleground."

"So, are we supposed to just back down?" asked Joan with more than a hint of annoyance in her voice.

"One of the things they never teach you in schools of education is how to understand political tugs and pulls. But you must have run into this kind of thing in your old job."

"Sure, but office politics was one of the reasons I wanted to get out of there and into a classroom. At Barker and Lloyd's, people were always looking for an edge, always trying to outproduce everyone else. I figured schools would be different."

"Maybe not as different as you thought," Margaret replied. "When I was in my second year of teaching, the teachers' union went out on strike for the first time in the history of the district. I went out with most of the teachers, but some of the veterans reported for work. I couldn't believe the hatred on the picket lines—the yelling and the name calling. I'll never forget talking to one teacher a couple of days before the strike. She told me that no matter what happened, she was coming to work. The way she put it was that the students were more important than a few more dollars in her paycheck. After it was over, a lot of her old friends wouldn't even talk to her; they avoided her in the halls. It took a *long* time for the school to recover. I knew I had to learn more about conflict and why it was so hard for people to deal with."

"So what did you do?" asked Joan with curiosity.

"I asked around and somebody finally told me about a book that had a couple of chapters on organizational politics. I was skeptical until I read them because I figured, 'Hey, I'm a teacher. This sounds like the stuff principals read when they want to know how to manipulate us.' But I devoured that whole book because suddenly a big light bulb came on. As teachers we all work in organizations, and half the time we can't figure out what's going on, because no one ever teaches us anything about how they work. We get a lot of stuff about psychology, teaching methods, curriculum—the stuff that's important in the *classroom*. But they don't teach us about *schools*."

"But why's that important if what you care about is what you do in the classroom?" asked Joan.

"Two reasons," said Margaret confidently. "The first is that the classroom is sort of a miniature organization in its own right. I was surprised when I started to think about it that way. Some things fell into place that never made sense before, and I started to see a lot of new possibilities for teaching and classroom management. Think about the struggle between you and Roscoe. People had tried plenty of coercion and punishment before, and he just kept getting more resistant. You started to get somewhere when you negotiated with him. The second reason is that how the school and the district work as an organization makes a big difference in your classroom. The debate over the inclusion policy is just one example."

"I'm still not with you," replied Joan with a puzzled look. "What's the connection between organizations and the inclusion policy?"

"Look at it this way. From a political perspective, a school is a collection of coalitions—a bunch of different groups, like teachers, administrators, students, and parents. Each group has its own beliefs, its own values, and its own interests. Every group wants certain things, but there's almost never enough to go around. Like, a lot of parents would like the school to revolve around the needs of their own child. As a teacher, you want to do everything you can for their child, but you also have to respond to all the other children in your class."

"But that means parents aren't really a coalition. They're a bunch of individuals," protested Joan.

"Sometimes and sometimes not," said Margaret. "Coalitions come and go, depending on the issue at hand. On some issues, the Pico teaching staff is really united, but right now, the inclusion policy is not one of them. Instead, you've got a couple of coalitions forming within the teaching staff, each based on different beliefs, different backgrounds, and different experiences."

"Maybe, but so far I don't see that you're telling me anything I didn't already know."

If Margaret detected the impatience in Joan's voice, it seemed not to bother her. She continued cheerfully, "O.K., but here's where I think it really starts to get interesting. If you want to understand what's really going on around something like the inclusion debate, you need a political map."

"A political map?"

"You want Pico to make a full commitment to the district's inclusion policy. Some people agree, others don't. To make a map, you start by asking who the key players are. Who are the people likely to make a difference in how the issue gets resolved?"

"O.K., there's the teachers. Some are with us, some are against us, and some haven't made up their minds."

"Right, and that last group could turn out to be very important," said Margaret. "Who else?"

"Jaime Rodriguez, and he's with us. We know that Superintendent Hofsteder is on our side. Then there are parents, but a lot of them probably haven't thought very much about the issue. Once they hear about it, they'll probably break into different camps, depending on how they think it affects their own children."

"Now we're making progress," said Margaret. "As you're talking about the players, you're also talking about their interests, what stake they have in the issue. If you go around and talk to a few people and ask some questions, you'll probably have an even better understanding. Then, you can actually construct a map on a piece of paper. On the right side, you could put the real conservatives, the people who are most likely to resist what you want. On the left, put the people you're pretty sure you could count on. Then, in the middle, put the folks who are neutral and might go either way. In this case, there seem to be a lot of neutrals, and that tells you something right away. They could make a big difference. One last thing. As you put folks on the map, put them higher or lower depending on how much power they probably have."

"I can already begin to visualize the map. The good news is we have some powerful allies, like the principal and the superintendent. But the opposition is pretty strong, too. So, we can probably win, but the war could be pretty gruesome."

"Once you're clear on the players and their interests, you can start to think about negotiation instead of armed combat."

Deep down, Joan felt very uncomfortable with all the talk of power and politics. She had studiously avoided the brokerage wars. Now, she wanted just to be a teacher and remain above the sordid world of politics. Yet Margaret made sense. "So, you're saying I need to draw my own map. Maybe so, but negotiation sounds like what you do when you're buying a used car, not when you're trying to help kids."

Later that night, Joan wrestled with Margaret's closing suggestion—that she meet with Phil Leckney. She found Leckney so frustrating that she wondered how they could even have a civil conversation. Yet she could not ignore Margaret's recommendation that she needed to work something out with the opposition to avoid tearing the school apart. She was also a little surprised that Margaret had suggested she talk with Phyllis Gleason before the meeting with Phil. But the most persuasive thing that Margaret said was, "If you're going to be consistent with your philosophy for dealing with differences among kids, don't you want to practice what you preach in dealing with your colleagues?"

To Joan's surprise, her meeting with Phyllis was a lot like her earlier meeting in which Heidi Hernandez had helped her get a better reading on Roscoe. From Phyllis, Joan had learned a lot about Phil Leckney and the other teachers who were on his side. Joan got a clearer sense of how much they could to do to block the new ideas that were so important to her and her allies. Phyllis also helped Joan get a better understanding of what "the opposition" was really concerned about. For example, Leckney was not so much against the new proposal as he was against anything that would make it difficult to stay on top of a classroom that was already very challenging for him. Pico's student body had changed significantly in recent years. The proportion of white middle-class students had declined significantly, while large numbers of poor, minority, and immigrant children were now filling the classrooms. The new students were a major challenge for Leckney and other veterans. Their teaching approaches had seemed to work fine with an earlier generation of students, yet were no longer doing the job. The issue for Leckney's coalition was not so much that they objected to the principle of inclusion, but they were fearful of anything that might make their classrooms more unmanageable and their jobs more stressful.

Margaret's offer to facilitate the meeting between Joan and Phil Leckney had turned out to be a good idea. It was clear that Margaret had been in similar situations before. She opened the meeting by focusing on the issue rather than on personalities or the feelings people had about one another. She also set some ground rules for the conversation. Both groups, she said, were committed to a quality education for Pico's students, but they had different views on how to do it. She suggested that they start by having both Joan and Phil each talk about their own views, insisting only that they focus on what they wanted for students, not what they didn't like about the other's stance.

As they talked, Joan was surprised to find more areas of agreement than she had expected. As the conversation deepened, Leckney acknowledged some of the challenges that he and others were grappling with. "It's changed an awful lot since I started," said Phil at one point. "When I was young, I felt like I came to teach and the students came to learn. That's not how it is any more. The neighborhood's more run-down. We've got a lot more poverty, a lot more single-parent families, more and more kids who barely speak English. We never used to have to worry about weapons or drugs in the school. Maybe I should have been trained as a social worker or something, but it's already tough enough managing the students I've got. What am I supposed to do with even more kids with behavior problems, learning problems, you name it? If we carry this inclusion thing too far, I think everyone will suffer."

As Joan acknowledged her own struggles with classroom management, she and Phil felt a bond for the first time. She learned from Phil that part of the opposition to her proposal came because it seemed to require every teacher to change right away when they were already feeling overwhelmed. Many of the teachers were genuinely doubtful that the new methods would really be an improvement. They all remembered other "improvements" that had flopped before and made things even worse instead of better. They feared, in fact, that the proposal might overwhelm teachers and lead to an overall reduction in the quality of instruction at Pico.

Margaret then raised the possibility of a pilot project as a way to learn more about how the new approaches might work. That would give the teachers who believed in the proposal a chance to experiment with it, while letting others have a chance to wait to see whether their fears and concerns turned out to be justified.

The meeting ended on a high note. Joan and Phil agreed that they both believed in the importance of student achievement and classroom management. Even though they disagreed on the impact of the district's inclusion policy, Phil agreed to support the idea of the experiment. Joan, Carlos, and a small group that called itself the "True Believers" formed to develop plans for the experiment. On learning of the group's name, some of the veterans playfully chose to label themselves the "Wise People." When one of them teasingly suggested that "True Beginners" would have been a better name for the other group, Carlos retorted immediately, "Does your group spell wise w-h-i-t-e?" The zingers hit home, but there was laughter on both sides. Joking and teasing became a playful way to acknowledge the tensions and build linkages between the two different groups.

With enthusiastic backing from Jaime Rodriguez, and no serious opposition from their colleagues, the "True Believers" plunged into their effort with great enthusiasm. Unknown to everyone at the time, the inclusion issue was only the tip of the iceberg in a larger problem of student discipline at Pico. While the pilot project moved ahead, new clouds formed on the horizon.

Student Discipline: Understanding Structure in Schools

One day in the faculty lunchroom, a group of teachers were surprised to find themselves talking about how much they missed Sam Shepherd, Pico's former assistant principal. Many teachers and parents saw him as the educational version of Attila the Hun, but his strong-arm approach to discipline had served its purpose, especially on the playground, in the cafeteria, and before and after school. Shepherd had taken early retirement only a month after Jaime Rodriguez became principal. Though the staff knew that Rodriguez had been instrumental in Shepherd's departure, few were critical of the decision. But Shepherd's absence was being felt. Teachers who had always sent disruptive students to face Sam Shepherd's wrath now had to fall back on their own resources, and many were struggling. Everyone was concerned about the recent increase in vandalism and violence at Pico. Teachers were frustrated about the graffiti that kept appearing on the school's once-pristine hallways and bathrooms. Parents were becoming alarmed, particularly after one well-publicized incident in which one student reportedly drew a knife on another one. As parents became more vocal, Jaime Rodriguez's office was sometimes the scene of shouting matches about what to do next.

It was during the same period that Pico began the process of implementing the district's new policy requiring the creation of a Local School Council in each school. Joan was pleasantly surprised to learn that, even though a first-year teacher, she had been elected as the council's first chairperson. She had become a candidate at the urging of Carlos Cortez, and was even more delighted when Phil Leckney also rose to her support. When she asked Phil later, his explanation was simple: "I supported you for two reasons. The first is that your business experience might be useful in this job. The second is that there weren't really too many people who wanted the job. I might as well tell you that some people may support you because they don't think you'll be very strong in the role, but I don't share that feeling."

At the first meeting of the council, Joan was not surprised when Mr. Rodriguez charged the group with looking into the worsening discipline problem. He offered them two alternatives as a way to focus their discussion. One was to hire an administrator to replace Sam Shepherd. The other was to develop a new schoolwide discipline program that would involve everyone—the principal, the faculty, and even parents and students—in implementing a shared discipline code. Joan was happy to have the discipline issue on the agenda, but she wished that Rodriguez had talked to her before presenting the two options to the council. Drawing on her experience at Lloyd and Barker's, she was pretty sure that her position as chairperson would be undermined if members of the council felt that the principal was running the show.

In subsequent meetings, her fears were confirmed. The council members represented various segments of the Pico community, including teachers, parents, and students. The group was diverse, particularly in their ideas about discipline. Despite Joan's best efforts, the council quickly bogged down in conflict and trivia. There were debates between liberals and conservatives, between teachers and parents, between those who wanted a single, schoolwide discipline philosophy and those who wanted discretion for individual faculty. Rodriguez attended every meeting and very often behaved as if he were chairing the council. Joan later heard informally that individual members of the council were having private meetings with Jaime to lobby his support for their own agenda.

Joan sensed that she was rapidly losing her ability to be effective as chair. Her experience chairing an informal task force in her previous job helped her see what was going on, but she was still not very sure what to do about it. She once again called on Margaret for help.

Margaret immediately understood Joan's concern. "It's not just you," Margaret said reassuringly, "the same thing is happening in lots of schools. Everyone's talking about empowering teachers and sharing decision making, but people are also telling principals that they're supposed to be strong instructional leaders. So principals often feel that they're the only person in a school who can provide leadership. We teachers often fall into the same trap by waiting for the principal to take the first steps. That makes it confusing in something like the council, where you have a teacher chairperson but the principal is there all the time. It's a dance in which no one's sure who's leading, who's following, and what rhythm you're supposed to be listening for. Some people are trying to waltz, and others are doing the rhumba. So you get a jumble of off-beat steps. I read an article the other day that called it 'Trouble in Paradise.' Shared decision making is the latest educational fad. The idea is good, but it's tough to make it work. What you have here is a structural problem, because no one's clear about who's in charge: you or the principal. People tend to figure that the principal is the real boss in a school, so they look to him for direction and answers. Jaime feels the pressure, and he does what a lot of administrators do: He sucks up all the responsibility. No one's at fault, but you need to do something to clarify the situation."

"Like what?" asked Joan.

"Well, Jaime's learning fast. I think maybe you just need to get his attention."

"How?"

"Send him a brief note telling him you're quitting as council chair."

"You're kidding!" said Joan. "I really want to be chair. I think I really have something to contribute."

"You're right," said Margaret, "and Jaime knows it. He needs you as chair at least as much as you need to be in the role. Trust me, as soon as he gets that note, he'll want to see you."

"Then what?" asked Joan.

"Tell it like it is, and don't pull any punches. Just make sure that Jaime understands that you're not blaming him, but you don't want to be part of a two-boss system that confuses everyone."

Joan was doubtful that the gambit would work, but she had enough confidence in Margaret's intuition to give it a try. Besides, she said to herself, I don't have a better idea. Her confidence in Margaret was soon reinforced. Within 24 hours of her sending a note to Jaime, he wrote back asking for a meeting as soon as possible. Joan went right away to Phyllis Gleason to make an appointment.

"Boy, does he want to see you!" said Phyllis with a knowing smile. "You don't need an appointment. Go right in!"

Jaime literally bounced out of his chair as soon as Joan walked in. He offered her the warmest greeting she could remember in a long time. Then he got right to the point. "Joan, I really hope you'll reconsider your resignation. If you quit now, I think it will really set the council back."

Remembering Margaret's advice, Joan knew that she didn't want to give in until she was sure that Jaime understood the problem. "Well, let me tell you why I resigned. For me, it's been a no-win situation. I've felt responsible for everything because I was elected chairperson, but everyone assumed that you were really in charge. Every time I tried to assume some authority, you did something to remind people that you were really running the show."

Joan had feared that Jaime would be surprised or even offended at her candor. Instead, he smiled reassuringly. "I think you're right. After I got your note, I talked to a colleague whom I trust, Brenda Connors. She told me the same thing. So we agree on the problem," Rodriguez replied. "We need to get clear about the council's role as well as the role of the chairperson. I've got an idea about how we can do it, but I need your help."

"Well, here we go again. You always have to be the one who comes up with the answers. Aren't you interested in my ideas?" asked Joan.

Rodriguez seemed briefly taken aback, but then he smiled again, and openly acknowledged that she had a point. "Look, Joan, I'm new and you're new. Maybe we both have a lot to learn. And right now you might not rate me as one of the most promising students you've ever seen."

It was Joan's turn to smile. "Now maybe we're getting somewhere. But I'm not going to be the chair unless we clear up some of the confusion about who's running the show."

"Can I offer a suggestion?" asked Jaime.

"Sure," said Joan, "if it's really a suggestion and not a command. You have a lot more experience in schools than I do, and I want to learn from you. But, sometimes your suggestions have sounded pretty forceful."

"Okay, okay, I get the message. You're the captain on this team. You and the council make the decisions. Actually, my suggestion is based on something that Brenda told me about. You decide whether it's a good idea or not. It's a process called CAIRO. It sounds like the capital of Egypt, but it's really a pretty straightforward way of trying to bring some of these structural issues to the surface."

"How does it work?" asked Joan.

"Well, CAIRO is an acronym. Each of the letters stands for a different kind of responsibility that someone can have in making a decision. Like there's someone—or some group—that is ultimately responsible for making the decision. They get the 'R' in CAIRO, because they're responsible, the monkey is on their back. A 'C' goes to anyone who needs to be consulted. 'A' designates someone who has to approve the decision. If someone just has to be informed about the decision, they get an 'I'. And they get an 'O' if they're just out of the decision loop."

"OK, I know what you're talking about. I ran into something similar in my last job. So, you set up a chart, like a matrix, with the different people along one dimension, and the different responsibilities along the other."

"Exactly," Jaime confirmed.

Joan liked the idea and probably understood the process as well or better than Jaime. But she worried that he would try to take too much responsibility in implementing his "suggestion." She stated her concern directly. "If we do it, I need to manage the process."

"That's a deal! Let me know if you want me to help. And, tell me the next time you think I'm stepping on your toes."

At the next meeting, Joan led the council through the CAIRO exercise. She explained the CAIRO acronym and distributed a matrix. First, she asked everyone to fill it out individually. Then they shared their individual perceptions. It was an eye-opener for everyone. It turned out that there were at least three different ideas about how the discipline policy was supposed to be developed. Implicitly, Rodriguez believed that it was his decision in the final analysis. Many teachers felt that the responsibility ultimately ought to be theirs, because most of the implementation would fall in their laps. Many parents felt that the council should be making the final decision. The group broke into laughter when a parent commented, "This looks a lot like the way my family works."

Afterward, Hilliard went to Rodriguez and said, "You know, the exercise helped. But I think I realized something even more basic today. I think the way the council itself is set up almost guarantees failure. It's the wrong group to hammer out something as complicated as a new discipline policy. The council is too big, it's too diverse, it's got too much to do, and too little time to do it. The CAIRO exercise showed that we have too many people who think they have the 'R'. But, if you think about it, there are really only a few people on the council who have a big stake in this policy. I think we should make them a group with responsibility for preparing a draft. They could consult with you, with the teachers, with the community, and with students. Then, if I understand how this site-based management is supposed to work, the council should retain final approval of the policy."

Jaime closed his eyes and clasped his hands to his lips. It was clear that he was thinking hard about what Joan had said. "You know, I think you hit the nail on the head," he finally said. "I kind of hate to admit it, but maybe the way I set this up was wrong to begin with. As you can tell, I'm still finding my way. A smaller group with a clearer task would have a much better chance of actually developing a workable policy. The council as a whole already has too much on its plate."

"Exactly. So the council makes its job easier by delegating this task. But, they have to give the subgroup a clear charge. I ran into the same thing when I was chairing a task force in my old job."

"I agree. Is part of the charge to make sure the major players all feel that they have been heard in the process?"

"Sure," said Hilliard. "Let me develop a proposal. I'll check it with you and with some of the council members. If enough people buy in, I'll get someone to bring it to the council."

At the next meeting of the council, Hilliard had arranged for a parent to propose a new design for dealing with the discipline problem. The parent said at the outset that the proposal had emerged from conversations among a number of people who were concerned about the problems the council was having. "The idea that we've come up with," she said, "is to create a task force to develop a proposal that they will then bring to us. In particular, their job is to consult broadly with the school community and to develop a proposed system that is viewed as fair, consistent, and workable by as broad a spectrum of the faculty, parents, and students as possible. Ultimately, their proposal would come to this group. We would assess how well they did the job we asked them to do. We would either approve the policy, modify it, or send it back to them for more work. Once we approve, the policy goes to Mr. Rodriguez, but he has agreed in advance that he will support whatever decision we make. He'll be consulted along with other people, but he agrees that he does not need to have an 'A' on this one."

Several council members glanced at Jaime, almost as if they were wondering whether they could believe what they had been told. Jaime acknowledged the glances and said simply, "The only thing I want to add is that I am fully behind this proposal."

During a long lunch break on a Saturday shopping excursion, Joan recounted the details of the discipline policy process to Margaret. Margaret seemed very pleased. "I hope you feel as proud as I do about what you've accomplished. Maybe it's your business experience. Even though you're a rookie teacher, you're already a model of what it means to be a teacher leader."

Joan beamed with pleasure. "Well, I really owe it all to you."

"No. Maybe I helped, but you really owe it to yourself. You brought a lot with you and you learn fast. I think you're in line for rookie of the year. I just hope a lot of our colleagues can learn from your example. If shared leadership is going to work at Pico, we're going to run into lots of challenges like the discipline policy. This is an important initiative. If we want it to succeed, a lot more teachers have to believe that they can take on some leadership."

"There's even another benefit," replied Joan. "In working out the confusion in the council, I realized that I have some of the same problems in my classroom."

"Which problems?" asked Margaret.

"Well, I was doing to my class what Jaime was doing to the council—taking on the all the responsibility. My students were constantly waiting for me to make all the decisions instead of taking responsibility for their own learning. It's not easy, but I'm trying to show them the difference between the 'R' and the 'C' in CAIRO. I'm trying to structure tasks where I have a 'C'—they should consult me for ideas and suggestions—but they have the 'R.' They're accountable for the decisions they make. I think that distinction is at the heart of what I'm trying to do."

Margaret thought for a moment, and then said, "Of course; whether we're talking about empowering teachers or empowering students, the basic issues are the same. I think you and I should do a schoolwide in-service on CAIRO and how it relates to relationships between students and teachers. In fact, I think it's important to get the parents involved in this. What do you think?"

"I'd love to! I learn so much every time we talk, but we haven't had that many opportunities to work together. The rookie and the veteran—we might make a great team."

"We already make a great team, because the rookie is already turning into a real pro."

Joan savored that comment throughout a quiet evening at her apartment. Larry was on another weekend business trip. Sometimes Joan was almost relieved if Larry was away midweek, because she usually had so much work to do anyway. But a Saturday night alone was an entirely different matter. She really felt like talking to him, but once again he had neglected to mention where he would be staying, and there were too many hotels in Atlanta for her to spend the night trying to track him down. "Oh, well," she thought to herself, "maybe it's just as well. If I tried to explain why I'm feeling so good about my conversation with Margaret, he'd probably just tune me out anyway."

The ring of the phone interrupted her reverie. "Sorry I couldn't call earlier, honey," said Larry's familiar voice, "but the meeting ran late. Anyway, I wanted to tell you that I love you. What's happening?"

"I'm Just a Great Teacher": Using Symbols to Revive the Spirit

When they hung that portrait of Phil Bailey on the wall, I was almost in tears. That may have been the single best event in all my years at Pico." The speaker was Phil Leckney, and the event was the "Fiesta de Pico," a gala celebration at the end of the school year in honor of two Pico principals, Jaime Rodriguez and his predecessor, Phil Bailey. Leckney was speaking to a group of his fellow teachers gathered at Andy's cafe after the fiesta.

"It was fantastic!" Joan agreed. "Before tonight, I'd never even seen Mr. Bailey, but I'd heard so many stories about him. It was almost like he was a ghost roaming Pico's halls."

"He was," replied Margaret emphatically. "That's part of why we needed the fiesta."

"Was this your idea, Margaret?" asked Carlos Cortez.

"No, though I wish I'd thought of it. I'm not sure who thought it up, but I know Phyllis Gleason masterminded a lot of it, with a good bit of help from Bill Hill."

"When the school's secretary and custodian put together the best party in years," replied Carlos, "it almost puts us professionals to shame."

"Maybe," said Margaret, "but the principal also helped in his own way. He gave it his blessing, then stayed out of the way and let Phyllis and Bill run with it. That was pretty daring for a first-year principal."

"Aren't you being modest, Margaret?" Joan chimed in. "I know you had a big role, too. I couldn't believe how funny you were in delivering the new principal's report card to Jaime. I can't remember when I laughed so much. When you told him he was getting an 'N' for 'needs to improve in opening sermons to the faculty,' we all just about fell out of our chairs. Even Jaime seemed to think it was funny."

"I could tell he wished his grades had come out a little higher," said Carlos, "but he was really pleased when you announced that he fully deserved promotion to second-year principal."

"And singing that song, 'If you knew Jaime, like I knew Jaime, oh, oh, oh, what a guy!' I've never seen him look so embarrassed, but you could tell he was proud."

For nearly an hour, people shared their favorite stories about the evening. The mood swung fluidly from laughter to tears and back to laughter again. It was Carlos Cortez who broke the magic spell with a more serious observation. "You know, this is the first time we've all had this much fun together in a very long time. We don't do this often enough."

"Yeah," added Phil Leckney. "And the sad part is that the celebration was for Bailey and Rodriguez—for our administrators, but not for us. How come we never do anything like that for teachers? Why should administrators get all the glory?"

His question struck a nerve, and a long silence spread over the group. Margaret Juhl, looking even more serious than usual, finally said in a very serious voice, "Phil, you just asked the right question. Maybe something's happened to all of us. Teaching used to be magic. It still is, sometimes, but it doesn't always feel that way. Every one of us has probably been at a party and met someone who asks us what we do. We get a little embarrassed and say, 'I'm just a teacher.' That's absurd! We ought to be the proudest people on earth. Yet we're taken for granted. A lot of the public seems to have the impression that we're not doing a very good job at something they think is pretty easy. We ought to see teaching as a sacred profession. Part of it is our fault. *We* don't take enough time to recognize what makes our job so special."

Joan agreed. "Margaret's absolutely right! This is my first year, and I've already lost some of the spirit I had in September. I love my students and feel good about how my class has gone, despite some rough spots. It's just that we don't take time as a group to laugh, share our stories, and have fun together. The funny part is that we did that a lot in my last job, and I kind of miss it. If something's missing for *me*, how does it feel after you've been teaching 20 years?"

The emotion in Phil Leckney's voice surprised everyone at the table. "I'll tell you what it's like for me. I feel more burned out every year. This year was a struggle just to get up in the morning and make it through the day. You all know I wasn't crazy about our new principal or about all the new ideas that he was pushing—with help from some of you, I might add. It's not that I'm a fossil. I don't resent new blood. God knows, I need a transfusion once in a while. But I need something so that I don't just coast my way to retirement."

"How about you, Margaret?" asked Joan.

"Maybe I pretend a lot," said Margaret. "My union responsibilities keep me busy, and I'm pretty good at mediating battles among different factions in the faculty. But when I close the classroom door, I sometimes wonder if I'm really making a difference. I used to be absolutely sure of that, deep down in my heart. Now, I sometimes wonder. Come to think about it, I could use a lift myself."

"Well," said Joan, "if we can have a huge celebration for our principals, why can't we have something like that for teachers? Are principals more important than we are?"

"Of course not!" Carlos responded forcefully. "What really matters at Pico is the same thing that matters in any school. It's what happens in the classroom, what goes on between us and our students. But it does sometimes feel as if that gets lost because we're so isolated. Joan, you've got a great idea! I love Jaime, and tonight's fiesta was wonderful, but we need to do something for ourselves as well."

Then to everyone's delight, Phil Leckney ordered a bottle of imported champagne. "In the Navy," he said, "there was always champagne whenever we launched a new ship. We're launching something just as important, and it deserves a toast!"

Throughout the summer, the group continued to meet, gradually transforming themselves into an informal planning team. Initially, they had wondered how Jaime Rodriguez would respond to their plans, but the strength of his enthusiasm made him one of their strongest backers. His only suggestion was that they add Phyllis Gleason to the group. "Phyllis knows how to do celebrations," he said confidently.

It was Phyllis who was the first to suggest that some students from Pico's past be included in the ceremony that the group was planning for the faculty opening day in the fall. "You know," she said, "we've had so many students that we might have written off who have gone on to do fabulous things. Take Carla Correa, for example. She's now the anchorwoman on Channel 5. Or, how about Benny Bernstein. Who would ever have thought that he would become a famous neurosurgeon?"

"Oh, come on," said Phil Leckney. "Not Benny! Anyone but Benny! He was the shyest, most off-the-wall nerd who ever graced Pico's hallways. We all thought he'd end up part of life's invisible woodwork. Benny does brain surgery?"

"Yes, Benny does—and very well," responded Phyllis. "Try another one. I'll bet none of you know which graduate of Pico is now teaching at Harvard University."

Several tried to guess, but no one hit the mark. "Charley Packer," said Phyllis finally.

That announcement seemed even more unimaginable to the veterans in the group than the idea of Benny Bernstein doing brain surgery. Everyone seemed so stunned that they could only roll their eyes in disbelief. Phil's almost inaudible whisper broke the silence, "Well, I'll be. I thought he'd be in the state pen, and instead he cracked the Ivy League. But suppose," he continued in a stronger voice, "those folks don't want to come back to Pico?"

"Nonsense," said Phyllis, "you'd be surprised!"

When September rolled around, the planning group was feeling nervous. They had invested an entire summer designing an opening day unlike anything in recent memory. Would it work? Would it flop? Would their colleagues think that they were crazy? Only Phyllis never seemed to lose her serene confidence.

Joan Hilliard heard some of the usual cynical murmurs as Pico's teachers assembled in the front corridor waiting for the opening day's activities to begin. What she overheard was not comforting. Few teachers sounded excited to be back, nor excited about what lay ahead. But when the doors to Pico's auditorium were opened and the teachers entered to take their places, the mood changed quickly. There were balloons everywhere, each balloon carrying the name of one of Pico's current students. The auditorium walls were plastered with words and phrases that described the profession of teaching at its best. Huge placards carried terms like "coach," "mentor," "guide," "guru," and "leader." There were pictures of previous students everywhere. The room was suddenly abuzz. Even the dyed-in-the-wool naysayers seemed overwhelmed by the banner across center stage. It said simply, "I'm just a great teacher!"

The room was still astir as people took their seats. In prior years teachers had often settled into a deadening funk in the face of a drone of announcements about procedures and policies. This time, a different spirit was in the air. But what was it, and what was to come next?

As the room quieted down, Jaime Rodriguez walked on stage. "Normally," he said, "I would give a speech. Hopefully better than last year's rookie effort. But this year, something really different is in store. And now, let the show begin."

A group of people walked on stage. Wilma Worthingham, a beloved teacher who had retired a few years earlier from Pico, was followed by several almost-familiar faces. As Wilma began to introduce each person, cries of recognition echoed across the room. "My God! Don't tell me that's Bernie," someone said. It turned out that the strange faces had names that were very familiar—at least to the veteran teachers. Each of the Pico alumni said a few words thanking the teachers for everything they had done, but it was Sid Holstrom who brought the crowd to its feet. "I was probably one of your worst, almost as bad as Charley Packer," he said. "And look at where I am now. And look at all the others who wouldn't be where they are if you hadn't helped them when they were at Pico. When you look at us, you see reflections of yourselves. We are your legacy. And we are only the tip of the iceberg. There are thousands more like us who owe you a debt of gratitude."

The ovation that followed seemed to last forever. It was not for anyone in particular, it was for everyone. As the din subsided, Phil Leckney walked on stage. His opening words shocked everyone present, especially those who knew him as Pico's resident cynic. "I am a Phoenix. I have arisen from the ashes of a burned-out teacher. This year the magic is there for me. If it can be there for me, it can be there for anyone here."

Many in the audience were stunned. Someone murmured, "What happened to Phil?" One of Leckney's long-time friends wondered aloud what he had been drinking that morning. Seeming to anticipate the surprise and skepticism, Leckney continued, "There may be some in the room who wonder if I've gone crazy. I have not. But I'm once again simply crazy about teaching. I have three years left before I retire. I'm going to make them the best three years I've ever had. I invite all of you to join me."

As Leckney left the stage to sustained applause, a young woman entered the stage. Few in the audience knew who she was. With her short, neatly coiffed brown hair and tasteful, light-blue summer suit, she looked as if she might be on her way to a job interview. She was too old to be a Pico student, yet seemed too young to be a teacher. The newcomer walked slowly and hesitantly, almost as if she wished that she were somewhere else. But once at the microphone, she spoke in a steady voice. "My name is Rosemary Pulcini. This is my first year teaching, and I'm proud to start my career at Pico. When I interviewed for this job, someone asked me who I admired most. At that time, I wasn't really sure. But I've had the chance to talk to some of you in the past few weeks and to hear many stories about Pico's students and particularly its faculty. I want to tell you that my heroes and heroines are all right in this room. I'm looking forward to teaching here for a long time."

The third standing ovation tripled anything ever before seen on opening day at Pico. The meeting was then adjourned to the cafeteria, normally a utilitarian space with an ambience of aluminum, formica, and a pervasive aroma of nondescript leftovers. Many teachers wondered if they had made the wrong turn when they found the cafeteria tables decorated with lace tablecloths and crystal candleholders. At every teacher's place was a crystal apple, inscribed with the person's name. The event was hosted with gusto by an enthusiastic group of Pico parents. Luncheon was an international buffet featuring dishes from each of the ethnic groups represented at Pico. No detail was overlooked. Margaret Juhl heard one veteran say, "This lunch is better than anything I've ever imagined, even at ten times the cost."

After the lunch, Margaret Juhl went to the microphone and said, "I came here 22 years ago because of the spirit I saw here. Over the years, that spirit has seen its highs and lows. But I think deep down it's always been here. This year, the Pico spirit is back stronger than ever. I would now like to introduce Pico's principal, Jaime Rodriguez. We are permitting him to say a few words because, frankly, we thought he deserved another chance after last year's opening-day performance."

Laughter filled the room, and Rodriguez was smiling broadly as he came to the lectern. All had been forgiven on both sides.

"What I have to say is very simple," Jaime began. "No school is much better or much worse than its faculty, and that's why I'm so proud of you and of this school. We have a great faculty here— some like Rosemary Pulcini who are just starting, others like Phil Leckney or Margaret Juhl who have served Pico for a quarter century. It's what all of you do in the classroom that produces the results we all were so proud of this morning when our graduates came back to say thank you. We can all see that Pico has a history that we can celebrate with pride. There have been ups and downs in recent times at Pico, and I spent much of last year just getting to know this place and its people. What I've learned convinces me that there are no limits to our future.

"As principal, my job is not to lead the charge, but to support and serve you so that you can use all your talent and energy to provide the best possible educational experience for our students. Together, we can bring new meaning to our watchword, Pico Pride. I want to introduce someone who can say all this much better than I, because she is one of you."

Joan Hilliard walked to the microphone. Those who were close could tell she was nervous. Her voice was soft as she began. "When I came here last September, I thought my four years in the business world would serve me well—and they did. But there were still times this past year when I wondered whether I could, or should, stick it out. Without a lot of help and support from many of my friends in this room, I would never have made it. But I did, and there's one thing I'm sure of now—I'm just a great teacher, and so are all of you!"

With that, she brought into full view a small bronze oil lamp. With a flourish, she lit the wick of the lamp. "Now, it's time to light the lamp of learning to illuminate our spirit for another year."

From the wings, the student chorus marched confidently on stage. Never had the school song sounded so good. And never had the cafeteria seen so many tears of joy.

Teaching and Leading: Balancing
Family and Career

The spirit of the opening day extravaganza lasted all the way to the holiday season. Throughout the fall teachers kept saying to one another that this was the best start they remembered at Pico. The school felt so alive and energized that people *wanted* to spend more time at work. Teachers who used to arrive barely in time to meet their contractual obligation found themselves arriving early to spend time chatting with colleagues and preparing for the day. A surprising number of parents commented that their children really seemed to be enjoying school more than ever before. People driving by the school at 5:00 on late fall evenings were often impressed to notice so many lights still on and cars still in the parking lot.

The planning team for the opening celebration (its membership more than doubled with the addition of new volunteers) continued to meet regularly under its new name, The Pico Pride Pack. They all agreed that the approaching holiday season was the perfect time for another teachers-only event—an ecumenical holiday party. Careful planning and a lot of work made their predictions come true. Phil Leckney, buoyed by his best year ever, provided one of the most jovial renditions of Santa Claus in anyone's memory.

Jaime Rodriguez donated what many thought must be the world's largest piñata. Margaret Juhl brought her still lovely voice to a medley of Hanukkah songs.

The committee had also arranged for a student event before the holiday recess. Heidi Hernandez wowed everyone with her ballet solo from the *Nutcracker*. The students went wild when Roscoe, dressed as Santa Claus and accompanied by his elf, Armando, missed the holiday piñata twelve times in a row. His final effort spread candy and small gifts across the entire cafeteria. Never had the first semester ended on such a high note.

Two weeks later, on a Saturday evening between Christmas and New Year's, Margaret Juhl received a tearful middle-of-the-night telephone call from Joan. "Margaret, the bottom just dropped out. Larry and I just had our biggest fight ever. It was the same thing he's been harping on for the last year. He said he was sick of playing second fiddle to my students. He gave me an ultimatum: Either I cut back on my work, or he's cutting out. I got furious, but I tried to stay calm. I just said, 'I don't tell you how to do your job. What gives you the right to tell me how to do mine?' He yelled back at me, 'That's it! I've had it!' He walked out and slammed the door behind him. I'm devastated. I thought we were starting to get past all this and that he understood how important teaching is to me, just like his work is important to him. It's like in his mind work is important if it's all about numbers and bottom lines, but not if it's about children! I don't know, maybe I'll never understand men. Maybe we'd be better off without them. But I've been crying since he left."

The conversation continued for more than an hour. Margaret mostly listened and tried to give Joan as much support as she could. Just before saying good-bye, they agreed to have lunch the next day.

When they met, Joan looked tired; her eyes were red and puffy. She acknowledged that she had cried a lot, but she seemed more composed than she had during the previous night's telephone conversation. As the two sat together over pasta at La Trattoria, the conversation gradually moved from Joan's breakup to a bigger issue.

It was Margaret who signaled the transition. "You know, Joan, as we were talking last night, some real painful stuff came up for me. The early days at Pico felt a lot like they do today. We all did things together, we enjoyed each other, and we did great things for kids. But it also took a big chunk out of our personal lives. You probably wonder why I've stayed single for so long. Partly it's because someone special walked out of my life, too. For pretty much the same reasons Larry did. I wish I'd been able to find a better way to balance teaching and the rest of my life. It's great for everyone to say teachers should take a more active leadership role, but not if it keeps them from having a life outside of school."

Joan was frowning. "Margaret, you sound just like Larry. Why do women have to do all the compromising and balancing, while men just go on doing their thing? If you're a man, you can be committed to your work *and* have a family. Women can do one or the other, but not both. Men get to work as much as they want, and we get the mommy track!"

"When you put it that way, it doesn't seem fair, does it?"

"It sure doesn't," Joan replied.

"Have you said all this to Larry?" Margaret asked.

"I've tried, but whenever we try to talk about it, it pushes too many buttons for both of us. We just get angry and fight. We never seem to get past that to have a real conversation."

"What you're saying is important. I don't have any answers, and I'm pretty sure that whatever they are, they aren't easy," replied Margaret. "It seems to me there's more than one problem here. One involves relationships between men and women. It's about sex roles and about what men and women need from each other. It's also about power and about what it means to be male or female. There's a second issue of overload—we all feel rushed and too busy these days. That one can affect any teacher, male or female. Right now, we're stuck—we don't know how to move on either issue."

"Maybe there's nothing we can do about it. Maybe that's just how things are." Joan looked and sounded discouraged.

"Do you really believe that?" asked Margaret skeptically.

The question seemed to mobilize Joan's more optimistic side. "No, not really. I'm just down after last night. In fact, an idea just came to me. How about if we talk about this stuff at the next Pico Pride meeting?"

"That's a terrific idea. Because maybe what we're talking about here is not problems, but dilemmas."

"What's the difference?" asked Joan.

"Problems have solutions. Dilemmas don't exactly *have* solutions, because you're caught between different values—like between commitment to teaching and commitment to family. It's not a tension that ever really goes away. You have to look for better ways to manage it. That's why it makes sense to talk about this with the Pico Pride Pack. Right now we're all dealing with symptoms. We need to get a better handle on what's going on and what we can do about it. I don't know any better way to do that than to talk with some colleagues who have the same concerns."

At the next Pico Pride meeting, Margaret and Joan presented the issues they had discussed. The nodding heads confirmed that others shared their concerns. On the surface, everything was going extremely well at the school, but something more troubling was bubbling underneath.

Phil Leckney led off the discussion. "I'll tell you one thing. You don't have to be female to worry about all this. I'm feeling caught in the middle myself. On the one hand, I've never felt better about my teaching. My classroom is running better than it has in years. The kids are learning, and I look forward to coming to school every day. But on the other hand, I miss all the spare time that I used to have. When I came to school at 7:30 and left at 2:30, I had time to do other things. I could work on my boat, spend time in the yard, and make a few bucks as a referee. I haven't been near my boat all year. The yard's a mess, so it's a good thing it's covered with snow. My wife nags me about not having the extra money."

"Wait a minute, Phil. I understand what you're saying," responded Rosemary Pulcini, "but I'm not sure you really got Joan's message—because you've got a wife. You have someone who takes care of the home front while you focus on your career. Joan and I don't have that. I know what she's trying to say. For me, being a first-year teacher is simply *overwhelming*! There's never enough time to do it all. Lesson plans, correcting student work, talking to parents, going to meetings—it never ends. And I'm not sure how long it's going to take before my husband tells me he's fed up. Your wife doesn't work, does she Phil?"

"Well, not now, but she used to before we had children." Phil paused and smiled as if to say that Rosemary's message hit home. Then he looked directly at Joan. "Maybe I'll always be a fossil in your eyes, Joan. You're right, my marriage is pretty traditional. But I wouldn't give up on Larry yet. Thinking back, I remember a time when I thought you were always on the attack, and I felt my best bet was to dive under some circled wagons. But all that changed when we started to listen to one another. If this old dinosaur can learn from you, I'll bet he can too."

Joan rose from her chair, walked over to Phil, planted a kiss on his forehead, and calmly returned to her seat. Phil turned beet red, and everyone was silent for a few moments before a wave of laughter spread over the group.

"You know," said Phyllis Gleason, "this conversation is a blessing. I've been worried for the last couple of months. I hear things. In one way or another, you all share a piece of the problem that Margaret and Joan are talking about. What's happening now is a lot like what happened in Pico's heyday. That was more than 20 years ago. It almost broke my heart. We had drinking, divorces. That's a *deja vu* I never want to go through again. It's not just you teachers feeling like this. I was talking to Jaime's wife last week. She was telling me she's worried because she never sees him any more."

"That's a good point," agreed Carlos. "We're not the only ones who worry about all this. As we get deeper into this stuff, it's important to include Jaime as well as other teachers and staff. How about if we invite Jaime to our next meeting?"

The group quickly accepted Carlos' suggestion. Rodriguez came to the next meeting and agreed that the issues deserved attention. He seemed as perplexed as everyone else about what to do about it. "It's really a dilemma. I've never been more proud of our school and what we're doing for our students. But the whole thing could crash if we all burn out."

"If we all have the same concerns," said Carlos, "how about a retreat to see if we can get to the bottom of what's wrong?"

"I think it's a great idea," said Jaime. "I'll talk to the superintendent about some funds for a schoolwide weekend retreat."

Joan responded angrily, "Now, wait a minute. Here we go again! If we do it over a weekend, it's another big chunk out of our personal lives."

"You're right, Joan," said Margaret. "It's a real Catch-22. But I think we're going to have to spend some time in order to get more. Another possibility would be to ask the district to cover a day's worth of substitutes. That way, we could spend an evening on Thursday, a whole day on Friday, and a half-day on Saturday. Is that a compromise that people would buy? I think the union could go along with that, as long as it's voluntary for teachers."

"Well, Jaime, it's up to you. You have to sell it to Dr. Hofsteder. Will she buy it?" asked Joan.

"I'm pretty sure she will, but I'm not going to ask for her support unless the faculty is really behind it," Jaime replied.

As it turned out, getting faculty support was relatively easy. Many shared the same concerns and worried about how long the school could continue at the same pace. The superintendent threw her full weight behind the idea. She and the school board were so pleased with what was happening at Pico, they did not want to see their lighthouse project run out of steam.

An expanded Pico Pride Pack planned the retreat. They agreed on a theme for the retreat—"Thriving and Surviving." As they wrestled with how to organize the time, Margaret Juhl offered an idea. "A few years back," she said, "I took a course on the principalship. It wasn't that I wanted to be an administrator, but I wanted to learn more about how they think. And I remember this one framework that's really been very helpful for me. It talks about four main issues that every organization, schools included, needs to address. One is to respond to people's needs and give them the skills that they need. The second is to manage politics and conflict effectively. The third is to create a structure that works, and the last is to develop a shared sense of meaning and commitment. I think each of these may be important to the issues of balance and burnout that we're trying to get at. What if we had groups working on each of them?"

"Wait a minute, Margaret," said Joan. "This all sounds *awfully* familiar. Haven't I heard this before somewhere?"

Margaret smiled. "You caught me. Those ideas have been in my mind during all conversations we've had over the past year. My questions to you were intended to help you sort through the situations you were running into so that you would have more options for how to respond. It worked that way for me, and I hoped it would work that way for you."

"Well, I think it did, even though I didn't really know it at the time," replied Joan.

"I don't know whether this conversation is a commercial or not, but listening to you gives me more confidence that this is a good way to go," Carlos commented.

Using Margaret's suggestion, the planning group broke the faculty and staff into groups charged with exploring one of four issues: (1) What in-service training do we need? (2) How can we deal with conflict more productively? (3) How can we use our time more efficiently? (4) How can we balance schoolwide cohesion and commitment with family and other outside obligations?

Despite some tense moments, the retreat was a huge success. A range of issues and feelings came to the surface, but they were almost always framed in a way that allowed the group to get below what people were thinking and feeling to the real reasons and to move forward. The group produced a number of new initiatives. It also identified areas where more information was needed. The efficiency team identified several structural avenues to make better use of time. One was to use team teaching to reduce duplication of effort. Another involved reducing the number of meetings that teachers attended. The overall impact was to free up time for individual teachers to do preparation and grading at school rather than taking it home.

The conflict group and the in-service groups collaborated to develop workshops on both alternative strategies for managing conflict and on techniques for time management. The cultural cohesion group concluded that another value should be added to the school's philosophy—sponsoring schoolwide events that included spouses, partners, and families to reduce the separation between work and personal life. The group also remembered what the original Pico Pride Pack had demonstrated about the importance of symbolic beginnings and endings. They ensured that the retreat ended on a high note with a series of skits that left everyone rolling in the aisles.

The Essence of Teaching: Leaving a Legacy

No one had expected it. Even though Margaret Juhl was close to retirement, everyone assumed that she would be around forever. The news that she had developed cancer knocked the spiritual wind out of everyone in the Pico community. Each day people waited for an update on her condition. Had the surgery been successful? Was the chemotherapy working? When would she be back to work? What will we do if she never returns?

Phyllis Gleason, in her usual role as hub of the information network, was a human hotline for news about Margaret's progress. Bill Hill served as the primary link to parents and the local community. School grapevines can distort the news, often specializing in worst-case scenarios, but Pico's gossip network was remarkably accurate and positive. It was as if everyone hoped that positive thinking would help Margaret's recovery and speed her return to the school she loved so much.

On a warm and sunny spring morning in late April, Joan Hilliard, Carlos Cortez, and Phil Leckney were the first to visit Margaret at St. Joseph's hospital. Phyllis Gleason declined an invitation to come along, saying, "The best medicine for someone who loves teaching as much as Margaret is a visit from a few of her closest buddies. I know Mr. Rodriguez feels the same way. He and I will be over at St. Joseph's in another day or so. Meanwhile, just be sure to call me as soon as you finish your visit."

As the three teachers walked down the shiny floor of a hallway that felt sterile and smelled of antiseptic, they wondered how Margaret would look and what her condition would be. As they entered Room 203, they were pleasantly surprised. Margaret was propped up in bed with a book, her wire-rimmed, half-circle reading glasses sitting crooked on her nose. The color in her face looked normal, although they suspected that her makeup had made it so. But the twinkle in her eye and the smile on her face when she saw them come in were genuine—the good old Margaret look that they would recognize anywhere.

"Joan! Carlos! Phil! So good of you to come. I told the doctors that if they didn't let me have some visitors, I was going to walk out of here against medical advice and find some company myself. Come on in! Sit down! Tell me the latest scoop from school. How's my class? Who's subbing for me? Are the kids behaving? Has Jaime been called in on a rescue mission yet?"

Margaret's visitors wondered if they had wandered into an interrogation chamber rather than a friend's hospital room. As the hail of questions continued, they looked in vain for somewhere to sit. With the overflow of flowers, plants, balloons, and gifts, there were no empty spots to be found. They were hard pressed even to find a place for the philodendron that they had brought as a gift from the faculty. Carlos started to move a huge bouquet of multicolored spring flowers from the chair by Margaret's bed in the hopes of clearing a place to sit.

"No, Carlos, don't move that one. That's from the kids in my class. Every one of them signed the card, can you believe it? Where did they ever get the money to pay for something like that? Come on, two of you can sit on the foot of the bed. Phil, lean against the sink. I want to be able to see you while you bring me up to date. So what's new at Pico? I'm dying to know."

Everyone winced at Margaret's choice of expression, but Carlos started the briefing, only to be interrupted by Joan with a story about Phil's failed attempt to play a classic "trick-the-inexperienced-teacher" prank on Rosemary Pulcini. Pulcini had caught on so quickly that the prank backfired and Phil himself became the butt of the joke. Phil blushed while everyone else in the room laughed uproariously. Margaret laughed so hard that tears rolled down her cheeks, streaking her rose-colored makeup. For the next half-hour, her visitors talked nonstop, sometimes with all three talking at once.

Margaret took it all in as if she were reconnecting to a vital source of energy from which she had been shut off for too long. As Phil was filling Margaret in on some of the latest community gossip via Bill Hill, Joan saw a hint of pain cross Margaret's face. She gently nudged her colleagues. "We could go on for hours and that might be just what Margaret wants, but I know the doctors will have our heads if we overstay our welcome." Margaret seemed both disappointed and relieved when her guests agreed that it really was time for them to go.

"Before you go, I want you to take all these envelopes with you. One is for my substitute, to give her some details of where to find things and some sage warnings about the students who are most notorious for driving off subs. The other envelope is for my students. I want Horace to read the first part to the class and then give it to Sally for the finale. Horace will be great in getting the funny stuff across, but he'd flub the last part. There's also a note for Phyllis and for Bill, so that they can help get the word around. And this one is for Jaime. He sent me a note a couple of weeks ago asking about some personnel decisions. Tell him I'm sorry I wasn't able to get back to him sooner. I know these things have been bothering him."

As Joan was wondering to herself whether there was any message that Margaret wanted to send to her colleagues, Margaret picked up the book that she had put down as they came in. "The last thing I want you to do is go by Barry's bookstore and pick up some copies of this book, *Among Schoolchildren*, by Tracy Kidder. I know a few people have already read it, but all of us should. It's about a teacher and her students in a school in New England. It says a lot about what's right and what's wrong in schools. Partly, it's about dedication and skill, but it's also about isolation, loneliness, lack of support. I find that every chapter really gets me thinking about teaching, and reminds me how much I really want to get back to my classroom. It would make me feel good to know that others are reading it too. In fact, the assignment for all of you is to read it before the next time you visit."

Joan, Carlos, and Phil all promised to do their homework. Each gave Margaret a hug and left carrying the envelopes that Margaret had entrusted to them.

"She looks great," observed Phil as they walked down the hall.

"She does," Joan replied, "but even though she seemed like her old self when we got there, she wore out fast. Did you notice the pain in her face just before we left? I'm not sure she's as good as she looks. I just hope she's going to make it."

"Don't even say that, Joan," replied Carlos. "She will. She's got to."

"Why do you think she wants us to read that book?" asked Phil.

"I guess we'll find out when we read it," Joan replied. "Let's stop by Barry's on the way home. It's only about four blocks from where I live. We can get the books before you drop me off. That way we can take them to school tomorrow."

When Margaret's three visitors arrived at Pico the next morning, they were in such demand that they felt almost like visiting rock stars in the presence of admiring fans. But the fans were not looking for autographs. They wanted to know how things were going with Margaret. Joan distributed the envelopes as Margaret had requested. Phyllis and Bill greeted theirs with such enthusiasm that Joan knew they could not wait to begin making their rounds to spread the news.

Two weeks later Joan was sitting in her apartment on a rainy May evening when the phone rang. When she answered, it was Margaret at the other end.

"Margaret, how are you? You know, you're still the only thing we talk about at Pico any more. Everyone keeps asking why we were all supposed to read the book."

"Well, that's part of why I'm calling. Joan, I'd really like to talk to you. I know how busy you are these days, but could you find time for another hospital visit in the next few days?"

"Is tomorrow afternoon too soon? Four o'clock?"

"That would be perfect. Just you, OK?" said Margaret.

Joan went to bed still pondering the meaning of Margaret's phone call. Nothing was said directly, but they had known each other so long that they often needed no words to understand what the other was thinking. Joan hated even to think it, yet she was almost sure that Margaret's call had not been prompted by good news.

When Joan arrived at Margaret's hospital room the next day, she was again greeted by the same cheerful Margaret, this time perched in the chair next to her hospital bed. Cards and writing materials were spread in a series of neat piles across her bed. "Joan, thanks for coming. I'm still writing thank-you notes. It's just amazing all the cards I've received. I was just reading one from a girl I taught more than 20 years ago, and I hadn't heard from her since. Let me clear some of this stuff away so you have someplace to sit."

"How about if I just move the stuff on this chair over to the window ledge?" At Margaret's nod, Joan sat down. "You're looking better every time I see you," said Joan, trying to sound as cheerful and convincing as she could.

"Well, the truth is I look a little more tired every time you see me. At least that's how I feel. Look, we've never tried to kid each other. The news from my doctor isn't as good as I'd hoped. I probably won't make it back to school this spring. This might have been my last year teaching." Margaret's voice was soft and there were tears forming on her cheeks, though hardly visible to Joan through her own tears.

Fighting the impulse to break down and sob, Joan came over and hugged Margaret awkwardly. "Please go sit down!" said Margaret. "There are some things I need to say."

Joan returned to her seat, fumbled through her purse for tissues, and struggled to compose herself.

"I've had a lot of time to think while I've been here—about my life, and even more about my career, and how teaching has touched every corner of my life in some way. I've been asking myself whether I would do anything differently if I had it all to do over. You tried another career before becoming a teacher. I never even considered other options. And there are a few times when I did something pretty silly or said something that hurt someone else. On these things I wish I had a second chance. But the thing I feel more sure about than anything else is that I made the right choice when I decided to be a teacher. I've started to think about what I'm giving back to a profession that's done so much for me."

Joan knew she should not interrupt, but the import of Margaret's talk about her legacy was too upsetting. Did it mean she was giving up? Joan blurted out, "Let's talk about the future, not the past."

Margaret smiled and responded calmly, "The future is exactly what I'm talking about. That's why I wanted to speak to you alone. You're very special to me, Joan. Have you read the book I assigned?"

"Every word. It was wonderful."

"I knew you'd like it. As I was reading it, it got me thinking again about the spiritual side of what we do. In earlier times, schooling was basically religious instruction. Somewhere along the line, we got confused and started to think of schools as factories instead of temples. As teachers, we have to hold on to the essence of what we're about. Otherwise, we stand to lose everything. Kidder had a beautiful way of talking about it. Wait a second, let me see if I can find it. OK, here it is. 'Good teachers put snags in the river of children passing by, and over time, they redirect hundreds of lives. There is an innocence that conspires to hold humanity together, and it is made up of people who can never fully know the good they have done (Kidder, 1989, p. 313).' "

"I love it! Isn't that what we were trying to get at with our celebration of teaching last year?" asked Joan.

"Yes, that was a great beginning, probably one of the best things we ever did at Pico," said Margaret. "But there's a deeper level of what we're about that we didn't quite get to. It's a level we're almost embarrassed to talk about—the spiritual dimension that makes teaching a calling. It's about values: the values we live by and the values we pass on to our students."

"Isn't caring the core value in teaching?" asked Joan.

"It's critical, but there are other important values that we often overlook. Take Roscoe, for example. You certainly cared about him, but it took more than caring. Being loved was not all that Roscoe needed. He also needed to master some basic skills and learn to set higher standards for himself."

"That makes a lot of sense. One of the toughest challenges I had with Roscoe was deciding when to tell him how much I liked him, and when to really push him to do better work and set higher standards for himself. So there are really two values in teaching?"

"We're only halfway there. In deciding when to support or push Roscoe, you also had to consider fairness for everyone in the class. Roscoe's like a lot of children these days. When they look around them, they feel the world is unjust. You agree. In trying to make it fairer for them, you can create injustice for others—particularly the kids in the middle. You know how much your students insist on fairness. They want a just classroom."

"That's what happened to me when we finally got Roscoe straightened out. Some of the other parents complained that their children were getting shortchanged," replied Joan thoughtfully.

"Can you begin to see that when you try to take all these competing values into account, there's always going to be tension. A classroom has to be caring, it has to be just, and it has to value performance and results. But even deeper than that, it has to be a place of hope. It has to have meaning and build faith."

"What do you mean by faith?" asked Joan.

"Faith is believing in things when everything tells you not to. It's believing in Roscoe even when his record tells you you're fooling yourself. It's convincing Roscoe to believe in himself even though almost no one else ever has. It's getting his parents to have faith in him and what school can mean for him. Even more important, teachers have to believe in themselves and in their work. That's where I think we've fallen down. Just pick up any magazine or newspaper. Listen to the conversations in restaurants. Think about how we teachers talk when we're together. The public has lost faith in us, and we've lost faith in ourselves."

"But what about the opening day celebration, or the holiday party? Weren't we on the right track?" asked Joan.

"Of course. They were both very important. So was the retreat, because it gave us a chance to talk about balancing conflicting values. For me, that's what makes the story Kidder tells so poignant. He said some things I'll never forget, and I want to make sure that people remember them at Pico even after I'm gone. That's why I wanted you to distribute the books. And I want you to promise me that you'll have the same conversation with your colleagues that we're having now. It'll be even more powerful coming from you, because you've tasted life on the other side. You chose to be a teacher after trying a career in business. I don't know why I feel so strongly about this, but I do. I have my own religious faith, and it's really a comfort now. But I'm also drawing heavily on my faith in teaching. I want to make sure others carry on these values while they have more time than I do to do good things for kids. Do you promise?"

The Torch Is Passed

Joan's promise reverberated in her head on the drive from the hospital to her apartment. When she got home to an empty apartment, she had an impulse to pick up the phone and call Larry, just to have someone to talk to. But she resisted as she remembered how rarely Larry had really understood her commitment to teaching. Instead, she picked up Kidder's book and started to read the final chapter one more time.

It was still dark when the sound of her telephone woke Joan early the next morning. Startled by the ringing, she looked at her clock to see that it was only 5 a.m. She was almost afraid to answer the phone. Her worst fears were confirmed when Jaime Rodriguez said, "Joan, she's gone."

"Margaret? Oh, God, no! What happened?"

"They aren't sure yet. The operation and the chemotherapy took a lot out of her, but even the doctors were surprised."

"I just can't believe it," said Joan, fighting back her tears. "I just saw her yesterday. She looked tired, but I just never expected this."

"I'm planning to have a brief schoolwide assembly this morning. I think we should tell everyone at once. I'd like to say a few words and then have a couple of teachers talk about her. I'm hoping to get someone like Phil Leckney or Vivian Chu—someone who's been at Pico and known Margaret for a long time. Bill Hill will be great because so many of the kids know him and trust him. And I also want you to say something, because I know how close you and Margaret have become."

"I don't know, Jaime. I'm not sure I can do it. I might just stand up there and cry."

"I'm not sure I can do it either," said Jaime, "but I figure I'm the principal, and I have to give it my best. And I'm pretty sure that if there's anyone Margaret would want up there, it's you. You're the last person at Pico who saw her alive."

"I just saw her yesterday," said Joan, crying softly as she spoke. "That's why this is so hard to believe. But you're trying to do too much too soon. Have the assembly today, but make it brief. We need more time to plan the right way to remember Margaret."

After a moment's hesitation, Rodriguez agreed and went to work to plan for a brief assembly, while Joan immediately began to think about how Pico might be able to celebrate Margaret's contribution.

The news of Margaret's death spread quickly, and there was hardly a sound as students and staff filed into the auditorium later that morning. The mood was somber, and only a few muffled sobs punctuated the heavy silence. Rodriguez was calm and controlled as he made a brief announcement of Margaret Juhl's death. He informed them when the funeral would be, and of the times when visitors could pay their last respects. He also announced that Pico would hold its own memorial assembly the day after the funeral. "And now," he said, his voice beginning to crack, "let's make the rest of the day just what Ms. Juhl would have wanted it to be—a day when everyone learns. That's the highest tribute we can pay to a teacher we all loved and admired."

Many staff and students sat in silence for a few moments, before slowly moving to the aisles. The only noise was the shuffling of feet, and the usual din of conversation gradually picked up as people moved through the hallways back to their classrooms. At the end of the day, several teachers remarked that even though students were subdued, they seemed very focused and eager to do their best.

On the day after the funeral service at Largren's Mortuary, Pico held its own celebration of Margaret's life. Jaime Rodriguez and the members of the Pico Pride Pack had spent many hours planning an event that would mirror Margaret's importance to the school. Without Margaret's steady hand and unflappable spirit, the planning process had little of the joy and humor that had always been there in the past. Even though everyone felt her absence as a gaping hole in the group's fabric, they worked with more intensity and focus than ever before.

Pico's memorial service was comforting, moving, and uplifting for everyone. Joan Hilliard felt almost like an emotional wreck in advance of the service and wondered if she could give the eulogy without breaking up. Yet as soon as she began to speak, the words flowed steadily, smoothly, and straight from her heart. Only after sitting down did she see the visible signs of her talk's impact—staff and students in tears all over the auditorium. It was then that Joan herself began to feel the full force of what she had said.

As the service drew to a close, Joan's mind wandered back to her first days at Pico, and especially to the time when Margaret first came into her classroom, just after Roscoe and Armando had destroyed her day. She beamed through her sadness as she reviewed how far she and the school had come since then. She thought about Roscoe, and how well he had been doing in Margaret's class before she died. Just as she began to wonder how well Roscoe would cope with Margaret's loss, she saw him enter the room with Heidi, Armando, and several other students pushing a wagon toward the podium. Perched unsteadily on the wagon was a large tree, its burlap-wrapped root ball hanging over the sides. As the entourage approached with its swaying cargo, Joan's eyes met Roscoe's, and she noticed the tears rolling down one of the largest grins she had ever seen on his face. It was different from the mischievous grin that she had seen so many times in the past. This was the earnest, self-satisfied look of someone who was confident he had done something really *right*.

The tree was not in the script, but a smiling nod from Phyllis to Rodriguez was the only signal he needed to welcome the group and invite them to the stage. To Joan's astonishment, it was Roscoe, not Heidi, who went up to the microphone. His words came out in a confident tone. "Ms. Juhl is going to heaven, but we don't really want to give her up. So we students took up a collection and bought this tree. We want you all to come outside with us and watch as we plant it in front of the school and water it. That way, we can keep Ms. Juhl's spirit with us and remember what she done for us."

Heidi Hernandez followed Roscoe to the microphone and read a poem that she had written. It was about a teacher who planted seeds of learning every day. All the seeds began to grow into beautiful plants, each different from the other. Over the years, so many plants grew that no one could even count them, but everyone could see how much more beautiful the world had become. Joan tried unsuccessfully to hold back the onrush of tears; she gave up as she noticed that she was not alone.

As she left the auditorium, Joan was approached by a man wearing the kind of dark suit that she associated with lawyers and bankers. "Excuse me," he said. "I'm a former student of Margaret Juhl's. She was the best teacher I ever had, and she made a big difference for me. I just wanted to thank you for the eulogy—it meant a lot to me."

"Margaret meant a lot to me, too," Joan replied. There was something about the stranger that felt very comforting to her, and she wondered who he was. "Have we met before?"

"I don't think so," he replied. "I'm Steve Riley. I'm a lawyer in Rosehill, and I do some work for the school board."

"Of course," Joan replied. "Margaret told me about you. She was very proud of you."

"It was herself she should have been proud of. I was a pretty confused kid when I came into her class. Anyway, thanks again for what you said today. Maybe we can get together some time and share reminiscences."

"I'd like that," said Joan. She hoped he meant it when he promised to call.

Six years later, Joan Hilliard found herself sitting with a new teacher, Francesca King, on the carved wooden bench under the oak tree in Pico's Margaret Juhl Patio. It was a beautiful September day, and Francesca had asked if they could meet somewhere away from her classroom. Joan automatically suggested the patio—whenever she went there, she felt Margaret's presence.

As Francesca started to talk, it was clear that she had wanted a setting well away from the chaos that had been her classroom that day. When Joan asked, "How's it going?" Francesca's words tumbled out in an almost-frantic stream.

"It's going downhill fast. Paul and Freda just made shambles of my lesson plan. I feel like I'm failing. I don't know, maybe I should quit now before it gets any worse. I've always wanted to be a teacher, but I never thought it could be this tough. I'm working just about all day and all night, but I still can't cope with my class, and my love life is going to hell. I feel like I'm drowning!"

Joan smiled as memories of her first encounter with Margaret flooded back. "This tree is beautiful, isn't it? It was planted here six years ago in honor of a wonderful teacher, Margaret Juhl. She was my best friend." Joan noticed the puzzled look on Francesca's face and went on. "You're probably wondering what that has to do with you. At about this point in my first year as a teacher, I was ready to quit, too."

"That's hard to believe," Francesca protested. "People say you're one of the best teachers they've ever seen."

"That's where the tree comes in," said Joan with a smile. "I wouldn't have made it through the first term if Margaret Juhl hadn't taken me under her wing. Tell me about your day. If we put our heads together, we might be able to figure out some ways to make it a little easier."

Epilogue: Diagnosis and Action
Signposts on the Road to Teacher Leadership

The dialogues between Joan Hilliard and Margaret Juhl offered a number of important signposts to observe on the pathway to becoming a teacher leader. The signposts are not prescriptions. They are guidelines that can help aspiring teachers develop their own artistry as leaders.

SIGNPOST 1 (Chapter 3)
Build Relationships on a Basis of Caring, Advocacy, and Inquiry

We often forget that individuals always bring their needs and their humanity with them when they come to work. They still need to feel safe, to belong, to feel appreciated, and to feel that they make a difference. Joan found herself troubled by tensions and misunderstandings in several relationships. Juhl provided a model of how to combine caring, honesty, and effective listening to build a more open and collaborative dialogue with both her student, Roscoe, and her boyfriend, Larry.

Margaret's model included three basic principles:

1. Open up communications and communicate a basic sense of caring and respect.

   Margaret noted that we often tend to avoid people or topics that risk producing tension or discomfort, but then we find ourselves in a bind because the problems do not go away yet we feel unable to talk about them. Margaret counseled Joan to engage difficult issues directly but to be careful to communicate basic respect and caring for the other person.

2. Ask questions and listen. Spend time with people. Listen to them. Attend to their feelings, concerns, and aspirations.

   When we disagree with someone, or are fearful about what they might say, we often stop listening. The problem is that when we shut down, they often shut down as well, leaving us in a stalemate. When conflict arose between Joan Hilliard and Phil Leckney, Margaret encouraged them to inquire into each other's views and to listen carefully to be sure that they understood. Joan and Phil were surprised to find that they had much more in common than they realized. This was a critical turning point: a relationship that began in conflict and tension eventually became one of collaboration and personal friendship.

3. Ask for feedback. Without feedback, leaders easily become blind to how they're really seen. If the feedback is surprising or negative, listen, acknowledge its importance, and share your own feelings.

4. Be honest, and advocate what you believe in.

   People need to know the truth and know where they stand. The problem is to communicate to them in ways that they can hear. The key is to tell the truth in a context of listening, caring, and trust.

SIGNPOST 2 (Chapter 4)
Map the Politics and Use Your Map

Juhl suggested three key questions to use in mapping the political terrain in a school:

1. Who are the key players? Who are the people, or groups, who care about the issue at hand? Will they care enough to support or oppose you? Who will, or might, make a difference in how things turn out? Whose help is necessary? Whose opposition is too important to ignore?
2. What is the interest of each of the key players or groups? That is, what stake does each key player have in this issue? What does each player want, and what can you do to help them get at least part of what they care about?
3. How much power does each player have? Who is likely to have the greatest influence over how this issue turns out? What is the source of power for each key player? Who could help if their power was mobilized? Are there any "sleeping dogs" better left undisturbed?

The answers to those questions make it possible to draw a map: a two-dimensional figure in which the vertical axis represents power and the horizontal axis represents position or interest.

With the map in hand, it's then possible to employ the strategies of effective and constructive politicians.

1. Clarify your agenda. You are clear on your agenda when you have both a vision of where you want to go and a strategy for getting there.
2. Build relationships and alliances. Work on building relationships with the key players. Spend time with them and find out how they think, what's important for them, and what they would like from you. The better your relationships, the more likely you are to build support and defuse opposition.
3. Facilitate the opposition. Talk to potential opponents. Listen to them and ask questions to make sure that you really understand how they think and what they care about. Acknowledge the importance of their perspectives. Encourage them to engage in a dialogue with the people they disagree with.
4. Deal openly with conflict. It is tempting but dangerous to ignore conflict or to sweep it under the rug in hopes that it will go away. People need a chance to voice their own con-

cerns and to hear other people's concerns. Otherwise, they usually get even.

5. Negotiate. As you get clearer on what you and other key players want, you can engage in conversations with them about options and possibilities for 'win-win' solutions. It is an ongoing search guided by the question, What can we do that will work for all of us?

SIGNPOST 3 (Chapter 5)
Align the Structure With the Job at Hand

People need to know where they're headed, who's in charge, what they're supposed to do, and how their efforts relate to those of others. Putting talented people into a confusing structure wastes their energy and undermines their effectiveness. Structural arrangements, like human needs, need continual attention, review, and realignment.

1. Clarify roles. Use the CAIRO process. Start by making a chart, or matrix, with the five CAIRO terms (consult, approve, inform, responsible, out) across the top, and roles (individuals or groups) down the side. Depending on the purpose, the list of roles might be longer or shorter. Next, have individuals or small groups fill out the matrix in terms of how they think the school currently works. They should do this for the particular kind of decision that is relevant to the problem at hand. Examples would include decisions about changes in curriculum, or decisions about disciplining students. Next, have everyone share their work and compare notes, which typically brings up areas of disagreement, ambiguity, or conflict. Even where there is agreement, the current role assignments may not be what the school needs. At this point, everyone should be much clearer about where the structural problems are. They can then move on to discuss the key action question: how should we allocate responsibilities for this kind of decision?

2. Design groups for success rather than failure. Make sure that groups have a clear charge—that they know what they

are supposed to do and what criteria will be used to judge
their success. Clarify to whom they are accountable: Who
is their client? What authority and resources does a group
have? For example, does the group have the authority to
make a final decision or merely to develop a proposal that
someone else will judge? Groups with manageable tasks,
substantial authority, and clear accountability succeed almost every time.

SIGNPOST 4 (Chapter 6)
Celebrate Your Values and Culture

It was only after Pico held a "fiesta" to honor the current principal and his predecessor that teachers realized the importance of
celebration in helping people feel the spirit and keep the faith. The
result was the "I'm Just a Great Teacher" celebration that became
a transforming event in Pico's culture. The following guideposts
can help you apply those lessons to your own school.

1. Learn the history. Cultures are created over time as people
   face challenges, solve problems, and try to make sense out
   of their experience. The present is always sculpted by powerful echoes from the past. Frequent glances in a school's
   rearview mirror are as necessary as having a vision of the
   future.

   The celebration of teaching reached back into Pico's history
   by identifying successful alumni and alumnae and bringing them back to witness what Pico had done for them.

2. Diagnose the strength of the existing culture. Some schools
   have very strong cultures: Beliefs, values, and practices are
   clear and widely shared; people are proud of the school
   and its traditions. Others have weak cultures: There is little
   agreement about or pride in the school's identity. Weak
   cultures often call out for change; they are an invitation to
   strong leadership. Strong cultures are the reverse; they resist change and reject leaders who are seen as enemies.

   The culture of teaching at Pico had once been much stronger
   but had weakened substantially in recent years. The celebration of teaching reached into the past to find themes

and values (such as "Pico Pride") and wove those into a new tapestry to speak to the current conditions.

3. Identify the cultural players. Who are the priests and priestesses? The storytellers and gossips? The heroes and heroines? Day in and day out these individuals reinforce and reinvent the culture. Priests and priestesses take confessions, give blessings when things go well, and provide solace in times of trouble. Storytellers pass on the lore and lessons of the past, while gossips keep everyone up to date. Heroes and heroines exemplify values and provide tangible role models. Phyllis Gleason and Bill Hill were so important at Pico because they played informal but crucial cultural roles.

4. Reinforce and celebrate the culture's strengths. Even in schools with weak or threadbare cultures, it is usually possible to find some things worth celebrating. Those stories, values, traditions, heroes, or heroines provide a vital starting point for updating, reinvigorating, and reframing the school's identity and culture.

SIGNPOST 5
Reframe

1. Reframing is a deliberate effort to look at the same thing from multiple perspectives. If you start, for example, with the political frame, ask yourself, "What is going on here politically? Who are the key players? What do they want? What kind of power do they have?" Once you have a political diagnosis, ask what you can do about it. "What options are available and which seem most promising?" Then, go on to other frames and go through the same process.

2. Reframing can help you steer clear of catastrophe and dramatically increase your chances of success. Consider reframing whenever (a) a problem seems impossible or you feel completely stuck, (b) you cannot make sense of something that is happening around you, (c) you seem to encounter one land mine after another, or (d) when you are about to embark on a major initiative. (Additional discussion of the reframing process can be found in Bolman and Deal, 1991.)

Conclusion

Berfore her arrival at Pico School, much of what Joan Hilliard knew about teaching was based on books, lectures, and a few gleanings from her experience in the business world. All of that was helpful, because anything was better than nothing. Over the course of her career, Hilliard was able to augment her book knowledge with wisdom that can only be gained from experience and practice. Although her appreciation for books and for new ideas and concepts actually grew over time, she also came to understand that ideas became useful only when she could figure out what to do with them. This book tries to illustrate the process of converting knowing-about into know-how. In the Juhl and Hilliard conversations, we have seen a combination of reflection on and dialogue about practice. Reflection is something that readers can and should do on their own, but its value can be immeasurably enhanced with help from others—friends, colleagues, and mentors.

You know, as do we, that a book is only a partial substitute for the kind of sustained and intense relationship that Joan Hilliard and Margaret Juhl formed with one another. But we hope that it can do some of the same things for you that Juhl did for Hilliard—raise provocative questions, offer new perspectives, challenge your thinking, and encourage your heart.

We hope that it will also encourage you to ensure that dialogue and mentoring are a rich and continuing part of your professional life. Teachers often feel isolated and trapped in their classrooms. They are surrounded and often overwhelmed by their students, each with a complicated array of needs and talents. Yet they often feel deeply lonely. They are starved for the opportunity to talk openly with other adults who can really understand what their life is like. Teachers can become collaborators; they can be allies and guides for each other. They can help each other through reflection and dialogue. Like Juhl and Hilliard, they can help one another create an inspiriting and elegant conversation.

Annotated Bibliography and References

Annotated Bibliography

A. General

Bolman, L. G., & Deal, T. E. (1991). *Reframing organizations: Artistry, choice, and leadership.* San Francisco: Jossey-Bass.

This book presents a systematic overview of our ideas about leadership and organizations, with many illustrations and examples from schools, colleges, government, and the private sector.

Bolman, L. G., & Deal, T. E. (1993). *The path to school leadership: A portable mentor.* Thousand Oaks, CA: Corwin.

This book tells the story of Pico School and its new principal, Jaime Rodriguez, as he searches for effective solutions to the many surprising problems and puzzles that he encounters in his early months. Like Joan Hilliard, he was fortunate enough to find a wise and caring mentor, in his case a veteran principal named Brenda Connors. Along the way we encounter Margaret Juhl, Joan Hilliard, and Phil Leckney, all of whom have even bigger roles in Becoming a Teacher Leader.

Gardner, J. W. (1989). *On leadership.* New York: Free Press.

If you could only read one book on leadership, this would be a very good choice. Gardner packs a lot of wisdom and experience into a highly readable and valuable book.

Johnson, S. M. (1990). *Teachers at work.* New York: Basic Books.

Johnson's book provides a very insightful view of how schools function as a workplace for teachers. She documents many of the barriers and frustrations that teachers encounter in bureaucratic organizations, and she offers helpful ideas about how to make schools better places for teaching and learning.

B. Power and Politics

Kotter, J. P. (1985). *Power and influence: Beyond formal authority.* New York: Free Press.

This book is written for corporate managers, but school leaders will still find it very useful. It is provides a very clear and comprehensive discussion of power and politics in organizations. Kotter's discussion of the "power gap" in administrative jobs, and his chapters on managing your boss, are invaluable.

C. Responding to Human Needs

Barth, R. (1990). *Improving schools from within.* San Francisco: Jossey-Bass.

This is Roland Barth at his best, offering a clear and compelling vision of how principals, teachers, parents, and children can work together to build learning communities.

Kouzes, J. M., & Posner, B. Z. (1988). *The leadership challenge: How to get extraordinary things done in organizations.* San Francisco: Jossey-Bass.

A stimulating and inspiring discussion of the practices of managers operating at their personal best.

D. Understanding Structure in Schools

Weiss, C. H., Cambone, J., & Wyeth, A. (1992). Trouble in paradise: Teacher conflicts in shared decision making. *Education Administration Quarterly, 28,* 350-367.

This provocative article documents many of the promises and pitfalls of shared leadership and teacher empowerment. In a national sample of high schools, Weiss found that there is a price to be paid for participative approaches to decision making, a price about which teachers are often ambivalent. The paper suggests that even in progressive schools, teacher leadership is conspicuous mostly for its absence, but we think it also shows how important it is for teachers to become more active leaders.

E. Symbols and Culture in Schools

Bolman, L. G., & Deal, T. E. (1992, Autumn). What makes a team work? Inside the soul of a new machine. *Organizational Dynamics.*

This article uses a famous case of an unusually effective design team to illustrate the symbolic and cultural elements that are critical to peak performance in teams.

Deal, T. E., & Kennedy, A. (1982). *Corporate cultures.* Reading, MA: Addison-Wesley.

A ground-breaking best-seller that first popularized the idea of organizational culture. The original—and still one of the best—overviews of what culture is, how it works, and how it can be shaped.

Deal, T. E., & Peterson, K. (1990). *The principal's role in shaping school culture.* Washington, DC: Government Printing Office.

A down-to-earth, practical guide to analyzing and changing school culture.

F. Ethics in Teaching and Leading

Bolman, L. G., & Deal, T. E. (1992). Images of leadership. *American School Board Journal, 179(4),* 36-39.

This article spells out the four values that Joan and Margaret discuss in Chapter 7, and relates them to four different images of what a school is: family, factory, jungle, and cathedral.

References

Bolman, L. G., & Deal, T. E. (1991). *Reframing organizations: Artistry, choice, and leadership.* San Francisco: Jossey-Bass.

Kidder, T. (1989). *Among schoolchildren.* New York: Houghton Mifflin.

Scriven, M. (1991). *Duties of the teacher.* Unpublished manuscript. Point Reyes, CA.